FOR ORGANS, PIANOS & ELECTRONIC KEYBOARDS

34

FIRST 50 MELODIES
YOU SHOULD PLAY ON KEYBOARD

T0039779

ISBN 978-1-70519-278-8

E-Z Play ® TODAY Music Notation © 1975 HAL LEONARD CORPORATION
E-Z PLAY and EASY ELECTRONIC KEYBOARD MUSIC are registered trademarks of HAL LEONARD CORPORATION.

Visit Hal Leonard Online at
www.halleonard.com

World headquarters, contact:
Hal Leonard
7777 West Bluemound Road
Milwaukee, WI 53213
Email: info@halleonard.com

In Europe, contact:
Hal Leonard Europe Limited
1 Red Place
London, W1K 6PL
Email: info@halleonardeurope.com

In Australia, contact:
Hal Leonard Australia Pty. Ltd.
4 Lentara Court
Cheltenham, Victoria, 3192 Australia
Email: info@halleonard.com.au

 # Registration Guide

- Match the Registration number on the song to the corresponding numbered category below. Select and activate an instrumental sound available on your instrument.

- Choose an automatic rhythm appropriate to the mood and style of the song. (Consult your Owner's Guide for proper operation of automatic rhythm features.)

- Adjust the tempo and volume controls to comfortable settings.

Registration

1	Mellow	Flutes, Clarinet, Oboe, Flugel Horn, Trombone, French Horn, Organ Flutes
2	Ensemble	Brass Section, Sax Section, Wind Ensemble, Full Organ, Theater Organ
3	Strings	Violin, Viola, Cello, Fiddle, String Ensemble, Pizzicato, Organ Strings
4	Guitars	Acoustic/Electric Guitars, Banjo, Mandolin, Dulcimer, Ukulele, Hawaiian Guitar
5	Mallets	Vibraphone, Marimba, Xylophone, Steel Drums, Bells, Celesta, Chimes
6	Liturgical	Pipe Organ, Hand Bells, Vocal Ensemble, Choir, Organ Flutes
7	Bright	Saxophones, Trumpet, Mute Trumpet, Synth Leads, Jazz/Gospel Organs
8	Piano	Piano, Electric Piano, Honky Tonk Piano, Harpsichord, Clavi
9	Novelty	Melodic Percussion, Wah Trumpet, Synth, Whistle, Kazoo, Perc. Organ
10	Bellows	Accordion, French Accordion, Mussette, Harmonica, Pump Organ, Bagpipes

CONTENTS

4	The A Team	78	The Imperial March (Darth Vader's Theme)
8	ABC	84	Jeopardy Theme
12	Addams Family Theme	87	Theme from "Jurassic Park"
14	All the Things You Are	92	Lean on Me
16	Amazing Grace	104	Let It Be
18	Autumn Leaves	97	Let It Go
20	Axel F	106	Linus and Lucy
28	Baby Shark	108	Minuet in G
30	Can't Help Falling in Love	110	Mission: Impossible Theme
25	Canon in D	114	My Favorite Things
35	Chariots of Fire	116	Over the Rainbow
38	Do-Re-Mi	122	The Pink Panther
40	Don't Stop Believin'	124	Shallow
44	Eine kleine Nachtmusik	119	A Sky Full of Stars
46	Fly Me to the Moon (In Other Words)	128	Smoke on the Water
48	Für Elise	134	SpongeBob SquarePants Theme Song
50	Gabriel's Oboe	136	Star Wars (Main Theme)
32	Hallelujah	131	Sweet Caroline
52	Happy Birthday to You	138	A Thousand Years
56	Havana	146	Tomorrow
53	Heart and Soul	143	VeggieTales Theme Song
69	Hotel California	148	Viva La Vida
62	How Far I'll Go	154	Wellerman
74	I Want It That Way	156	What a Wonderful World
81	Imagine	158	You Are My Sunshine

The A Team

Registration 4
Rhythm: Folk or Ballad

Words and Music by
Ed Sheeran

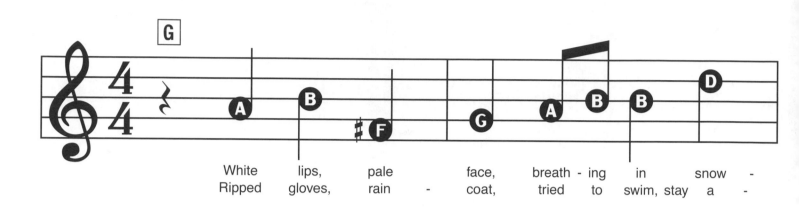

White lips, pale face, breath - ing in snow -
Ripped gloves, rain - coat, tried to swim, stay a -

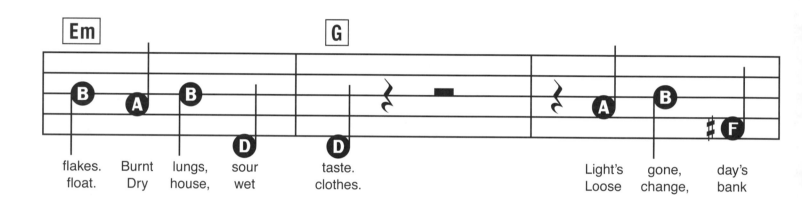

flakes. Burnt lungs, sour taste.
float. Dry house, wet clothes.

Light's gone, day's
Loose change, bank

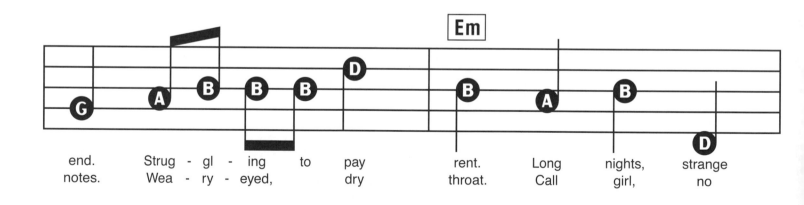

end. Strug - gl - ing to pay rent. Long nights, strange
notes. Wea - ry - eyed, dry throat. Call girl, no

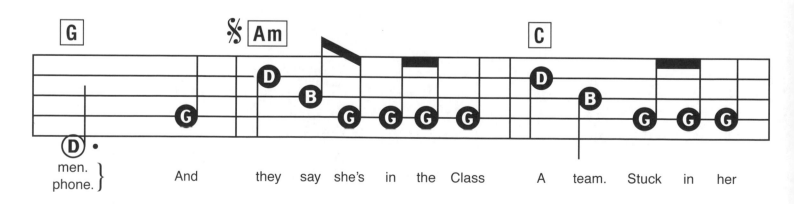

men.
phone.

And they say she's in the Class A team. Stuck in her

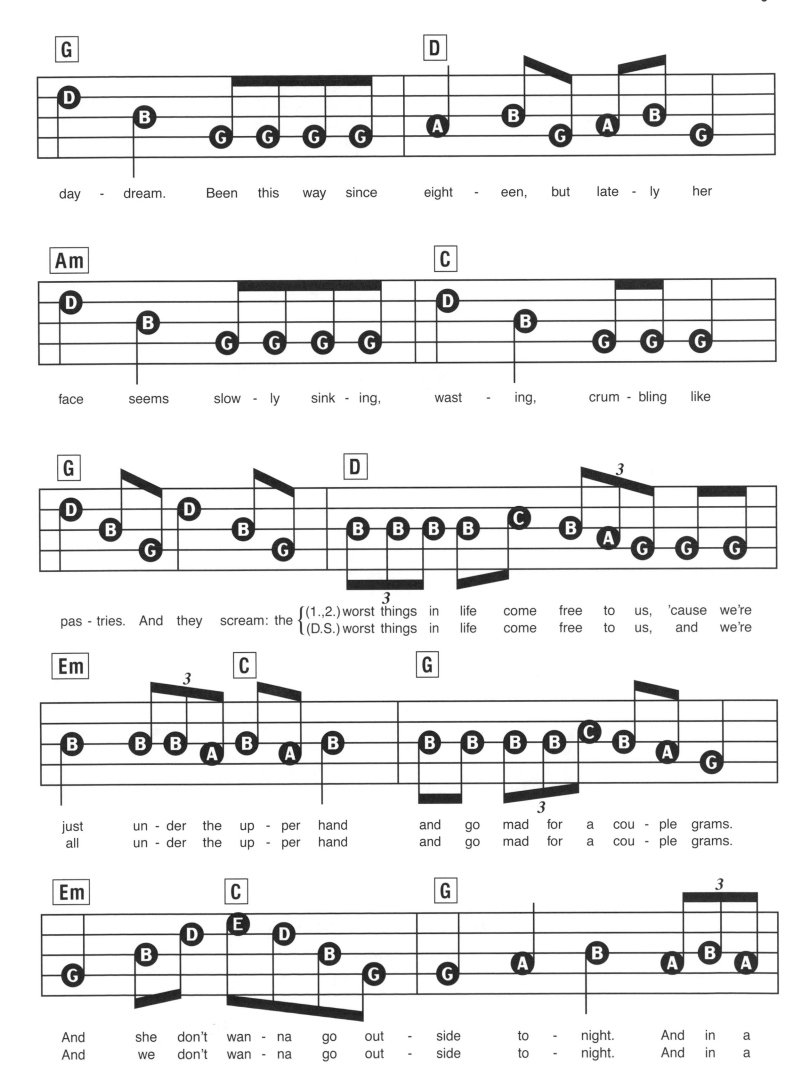

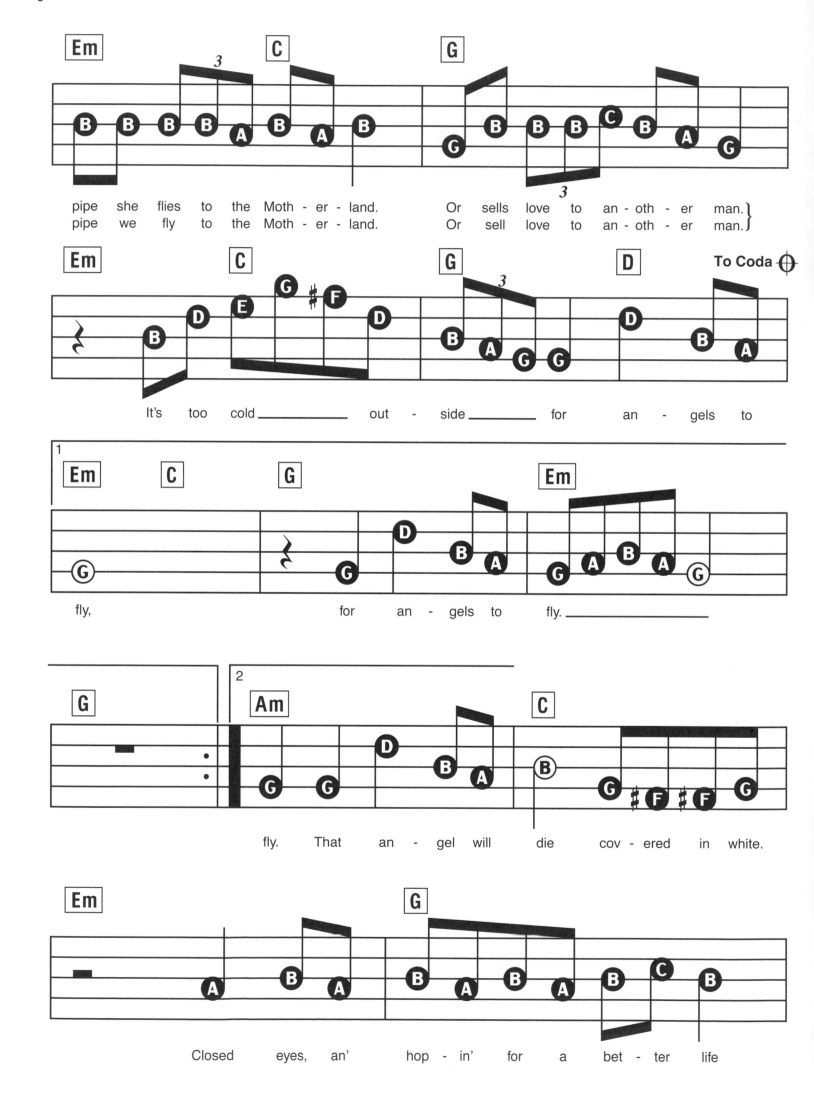

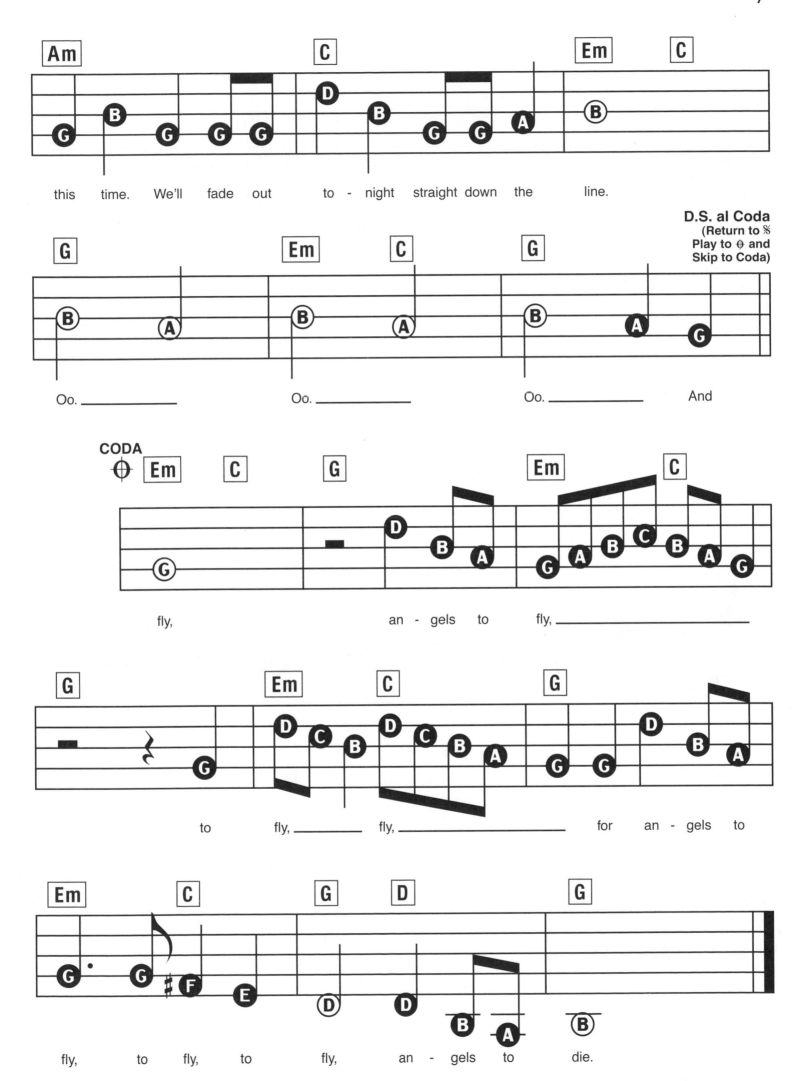

ABC

Registration 9
Rhythm: Rock

Words and Music by Alphonso Mizell,
Frederick Perren, Deke Richards and Berry Gordy

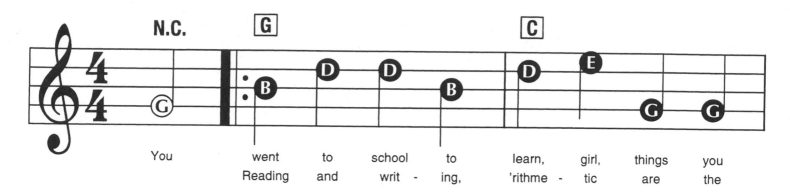

You
Reading

went   to   school   to   learn, girl,   things   you
and   writ - ing,   'rithme - tic   are   the

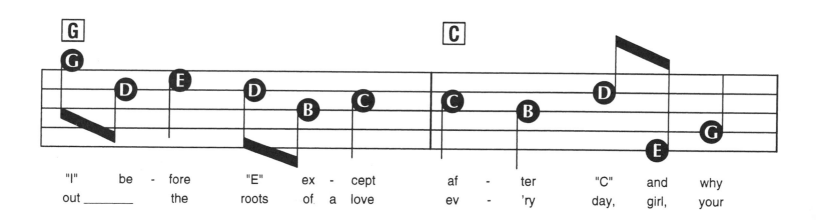

nev - er,   nev - er   knew   be - fore.   like _____
branch - es   of   the   learn - ing   tree.   With _____

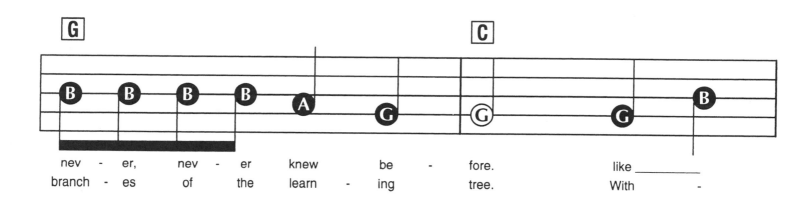

"I"   be - fore   "E"   ex - cept   af - ter   "C"   and   why
out _____   the   roots   of   a   love   ev - 'ry   day, girl,   your

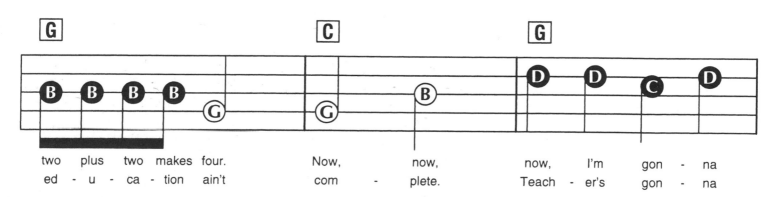

two   plus   two   makes   four.   Now,   now,   now,   I'm   gon - na
ed - u - ca - tion   ain't   com - plete.   Teach - er's   gon - na

9

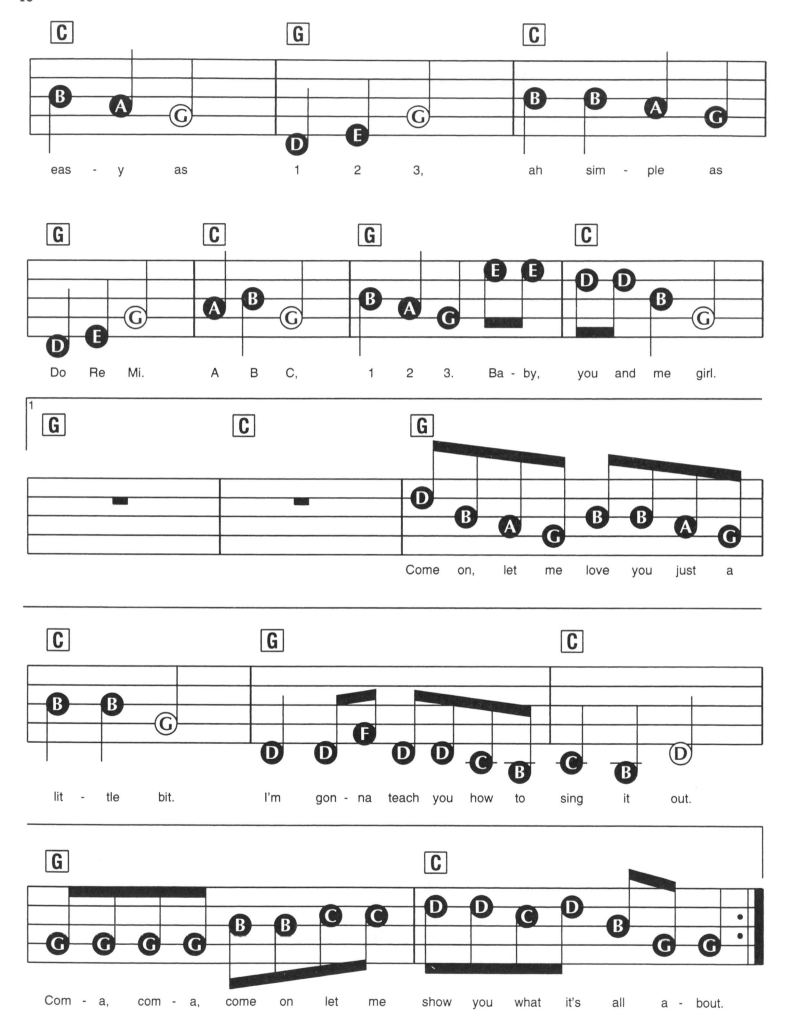

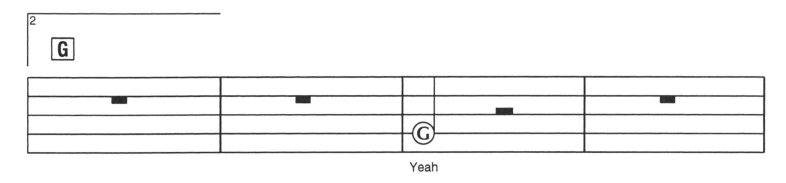

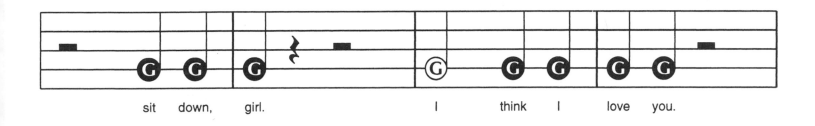

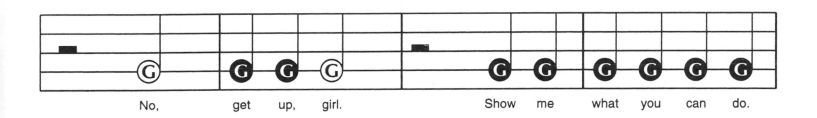

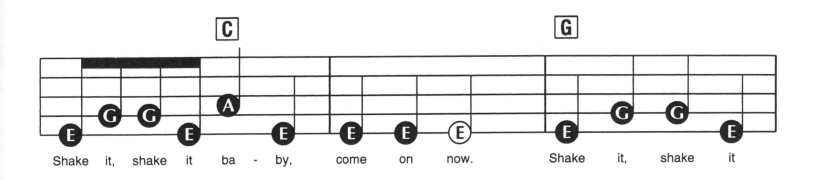

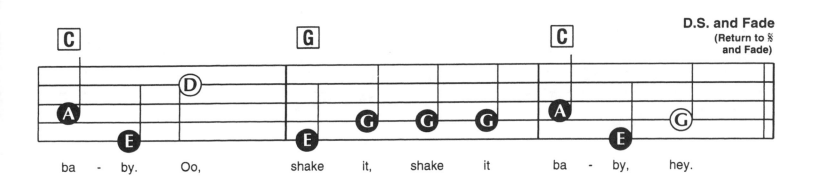

Addams Family Theme
Theme from the TV Show and Movie

Registration 9
Rhythm: Shuffle or Swing

Music and Lyrics by
Vic Mizzy

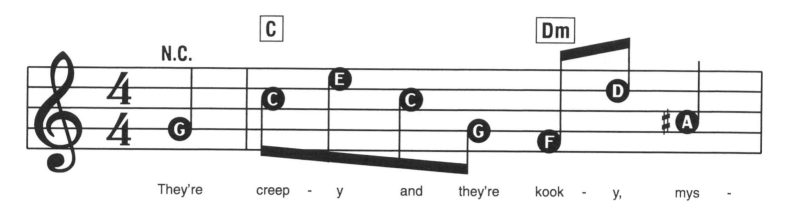

They're creep - y and they're kook - y, mys -

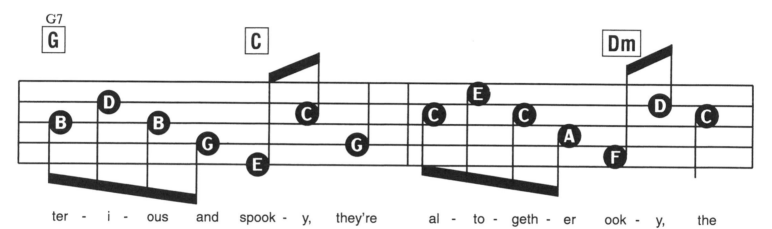

ter - i - ous and spook - y, they're al - to - geth - er ook - y, the

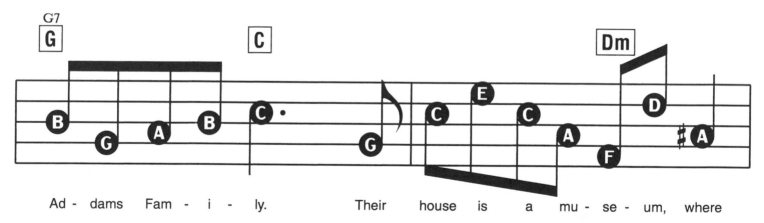

Ad - dams Fam - i - ly. Their house is a mu - se - um, where

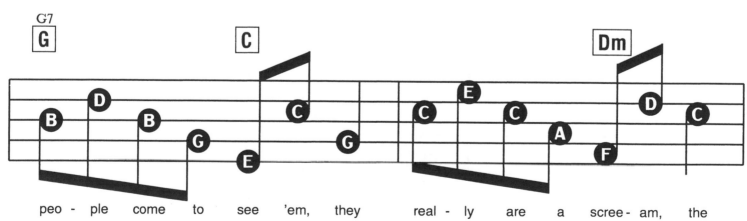

peo - ple come to see 'em, they real - ly are a scree - am, the

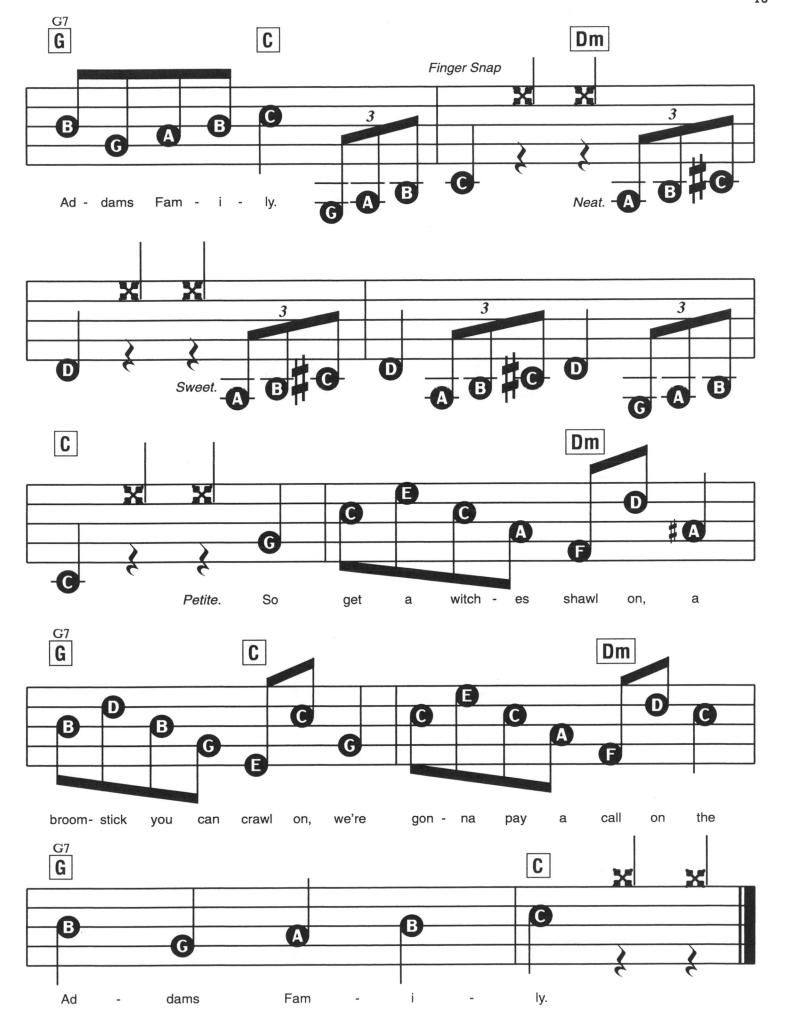

All the Things You Are
from VERY WARM FOR MAY

Registration 2
Rhythm: Ballad or Swing

Lyrics by Oscar Hammerstein II
Music by Jerome Kern

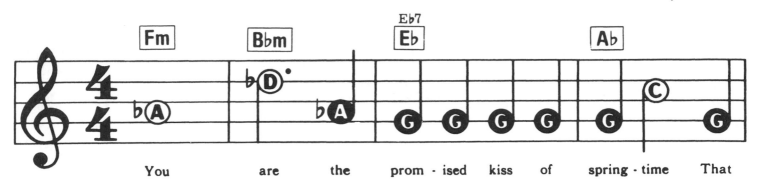

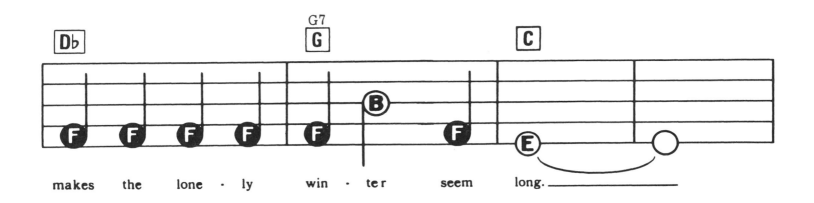

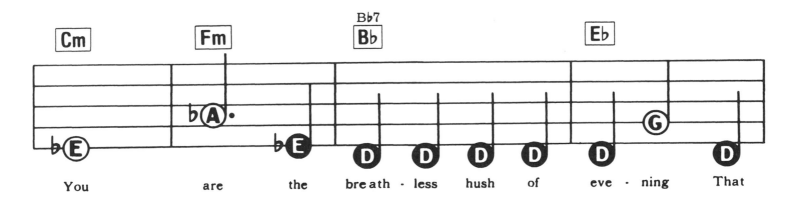

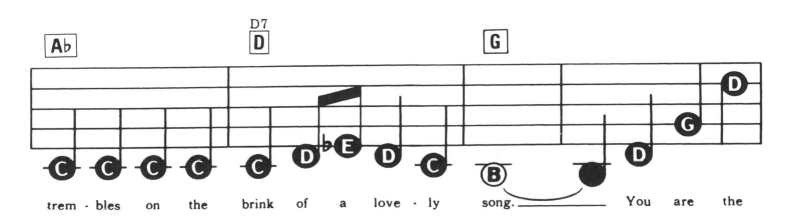

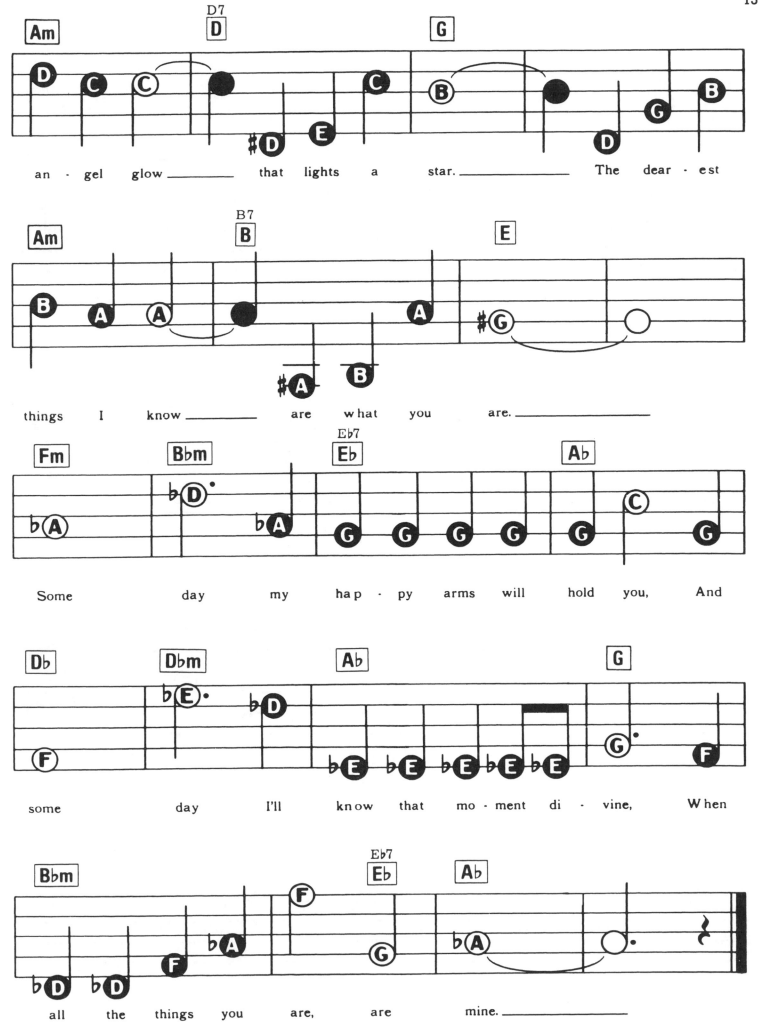

Amazing Grace

Registration 6
Rhythm: Waltz

Words by John Newton
Traditional American Melody

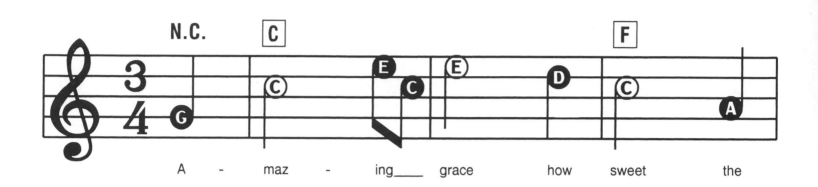

A - maz - ing____ grace how sweet the

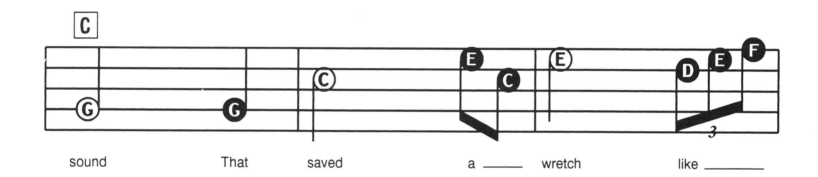

sound   That   saved   a ____ wretch   like _____

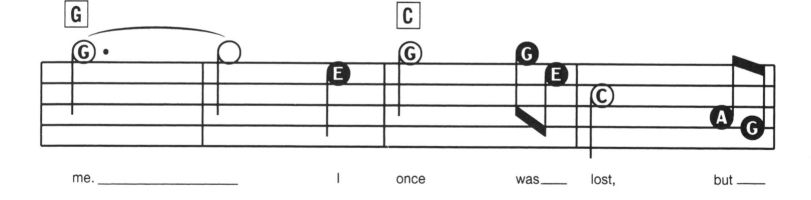

me. _____   I   once   was____ lost,   but ____

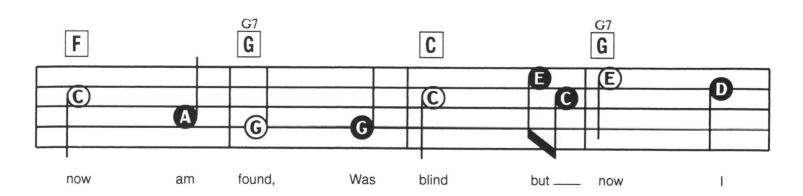

now   am   found,   Was   blind   but ____ now   I

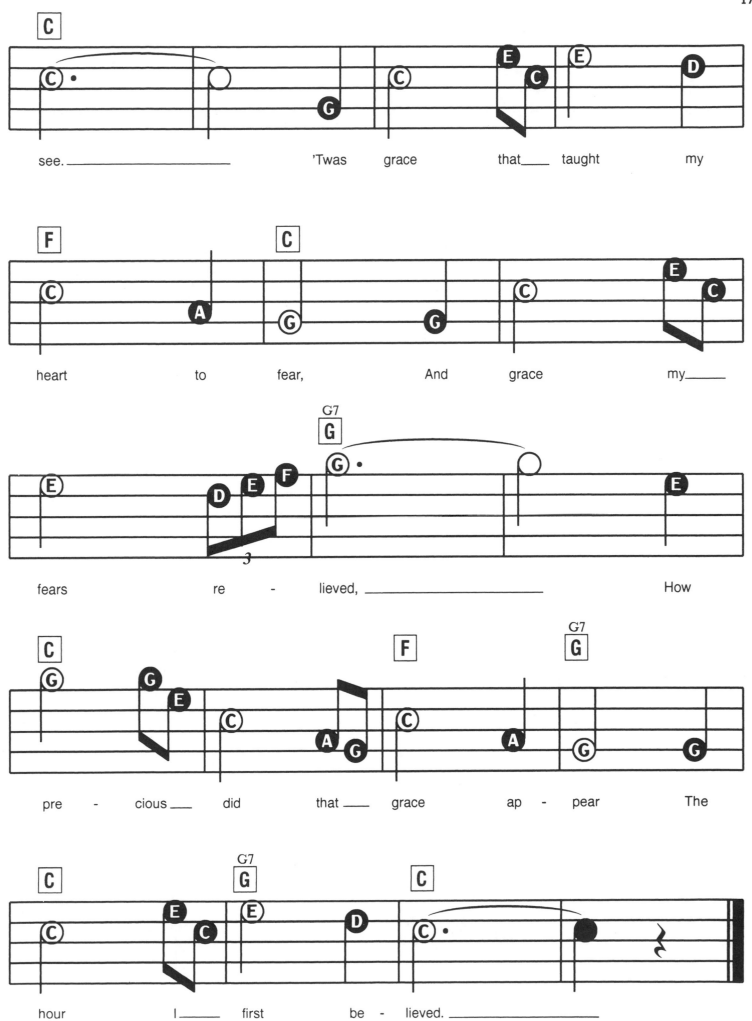

Autumn Leaves

Registration 2
Rhythm: Fox Trot or Ballad

English lyric by Johnny Mercer
French lyric by Jacques Prevert
Music by Joseph Kosma

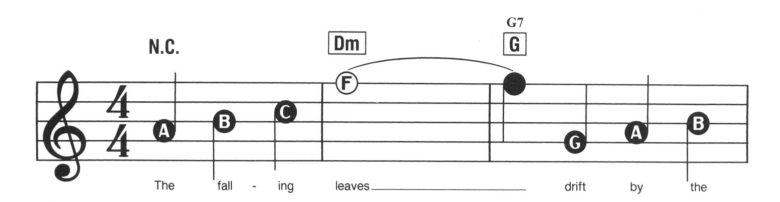

The fall - ing leaves _____ drift by the

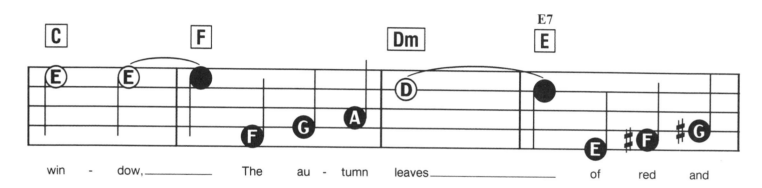

win - dow, _____ The au - tumn leaves _____ of red and

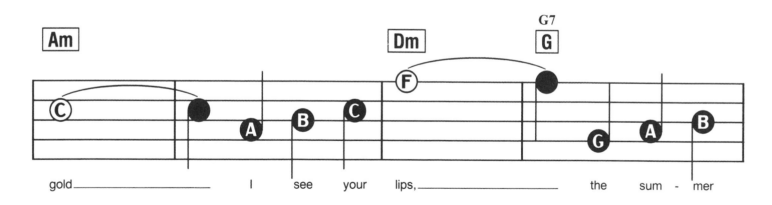

gold _____ I see your lips, _____ the sum - mer

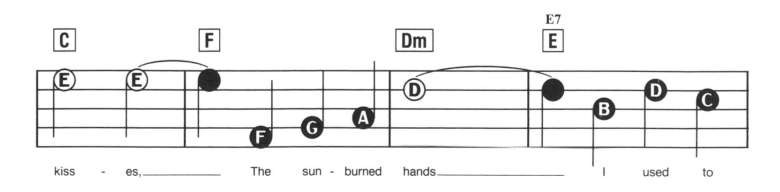

kiss - es, _____ The sun - burned hands _____ I used to

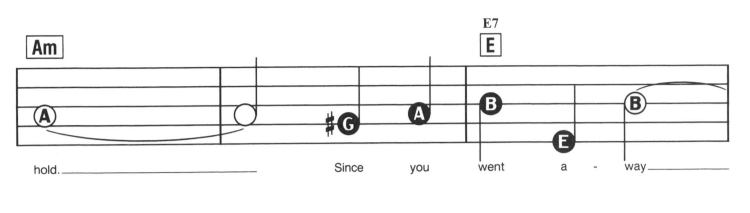

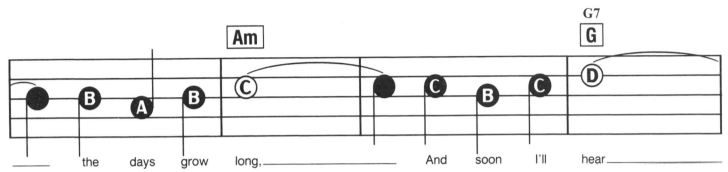

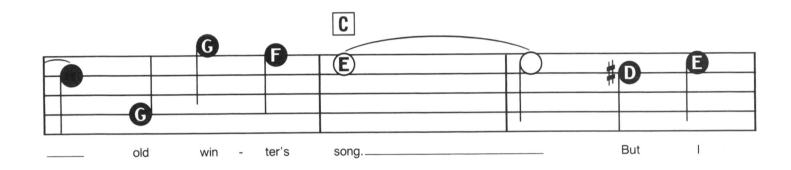

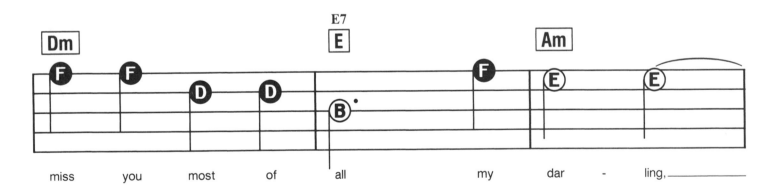

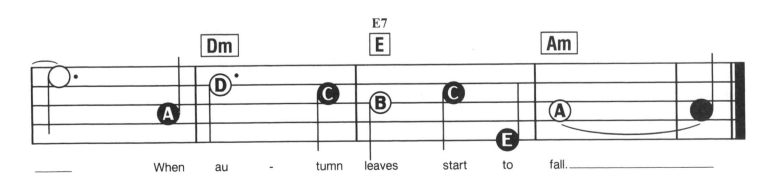

Axel F
Theme from the Paramount Motion Picture BEVERLY HILLS COP

Registration 5
Rhythm: Rock or 16-Beat

By Harold Faltermeyer

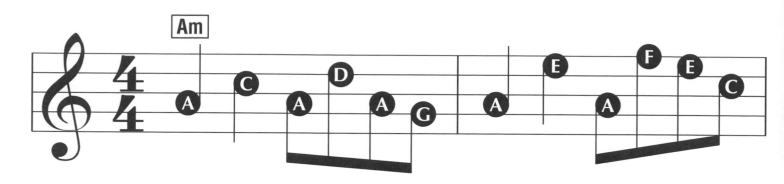

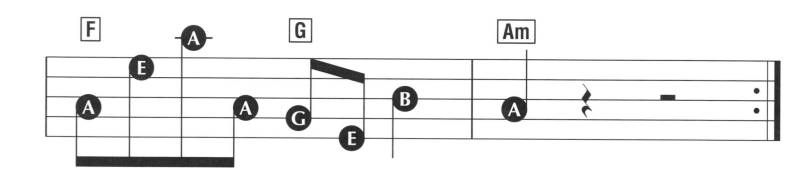

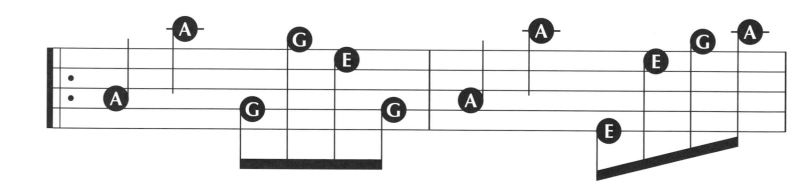

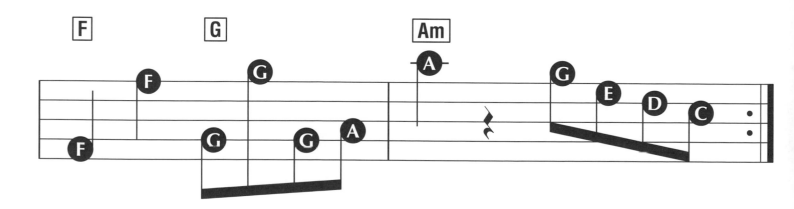

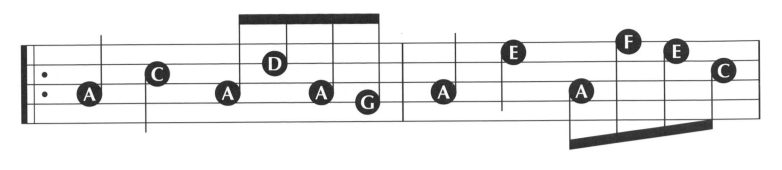

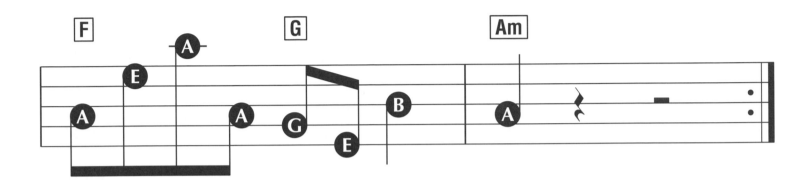

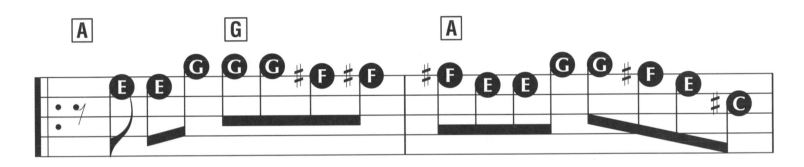

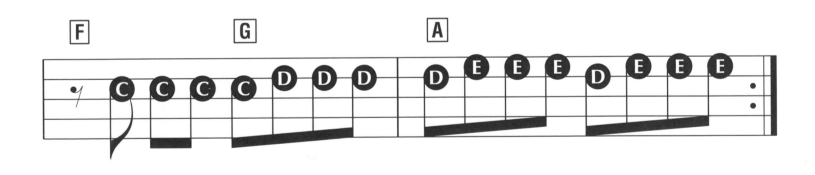

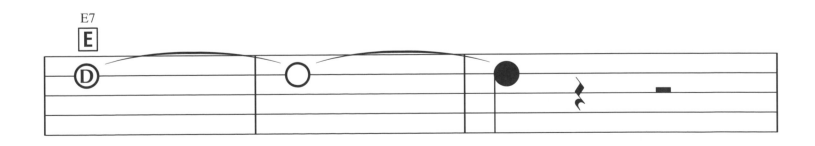

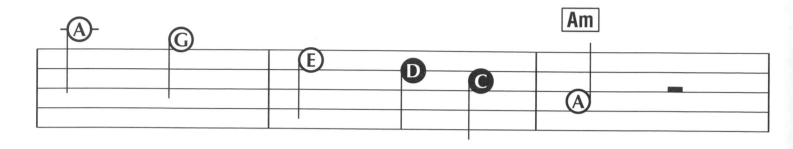

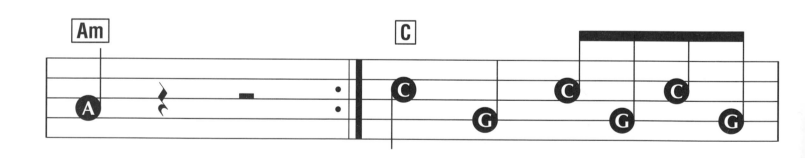

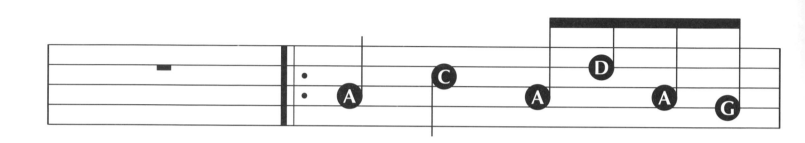

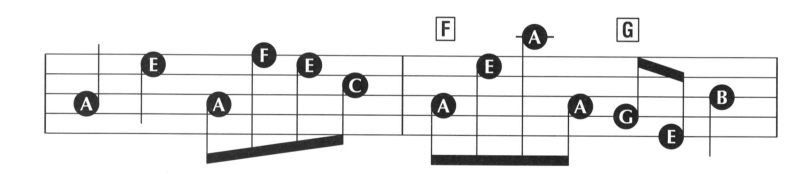

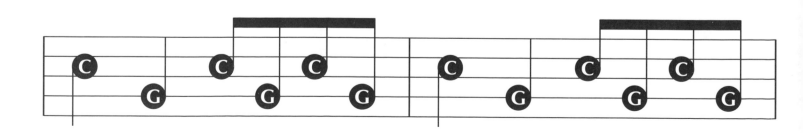

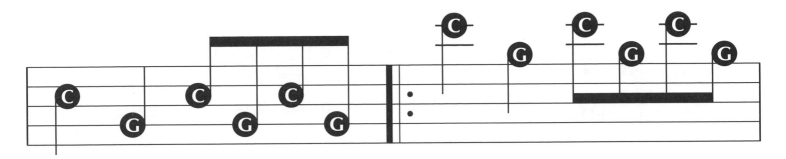

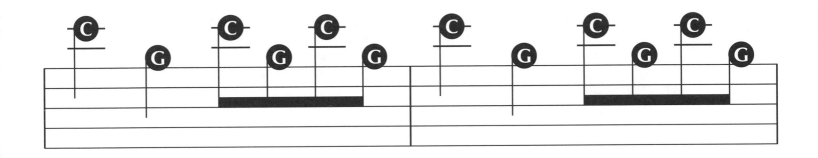

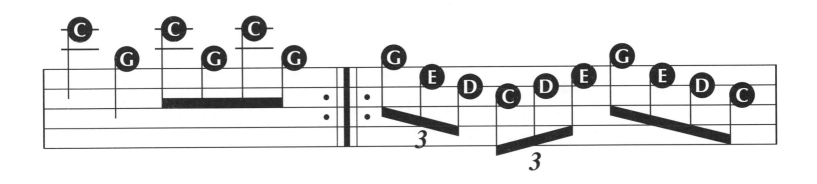

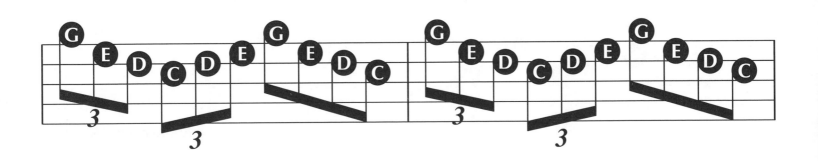

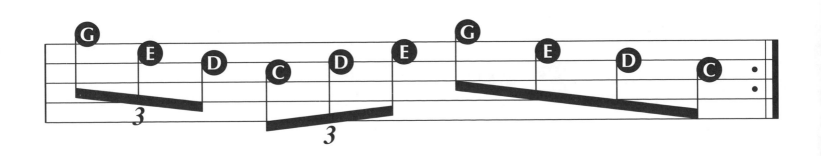

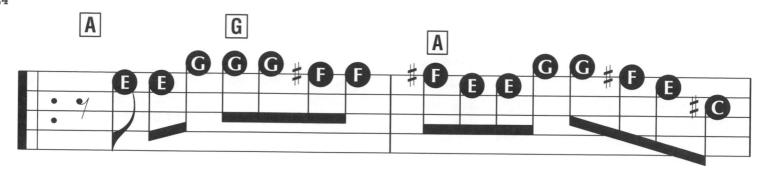

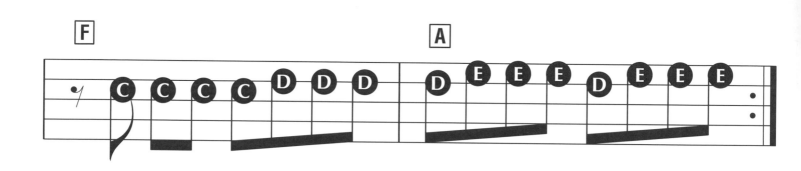

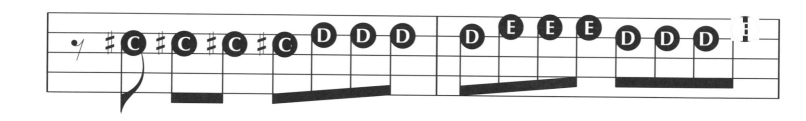

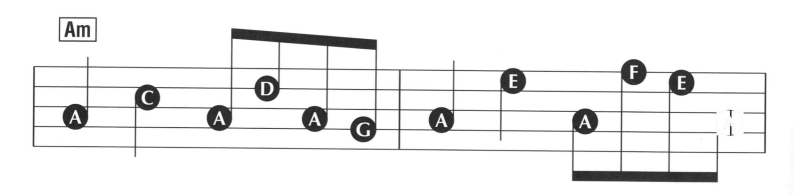

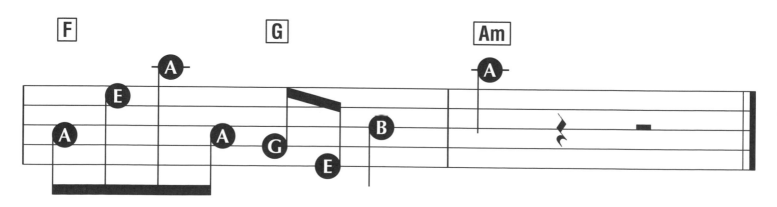

Canon in D

Registration 3
Rhythm: 8-Beat or None

By Johann Pachelbel

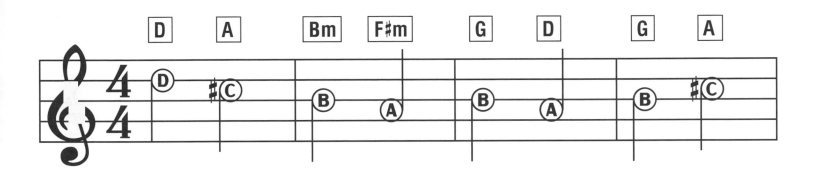

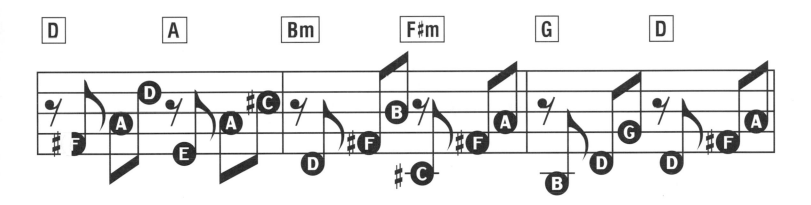

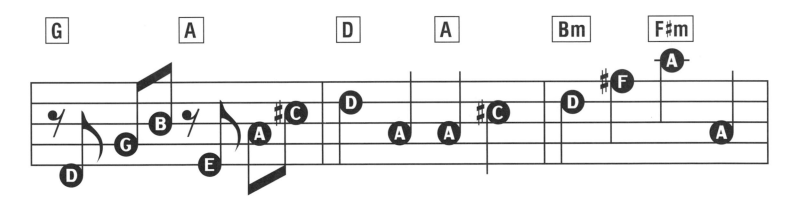

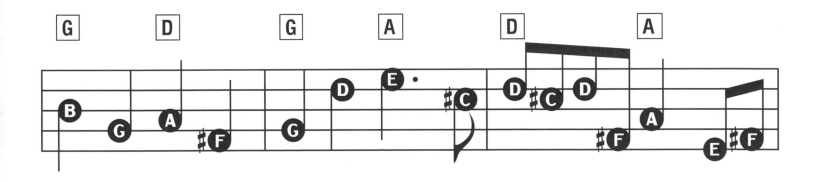

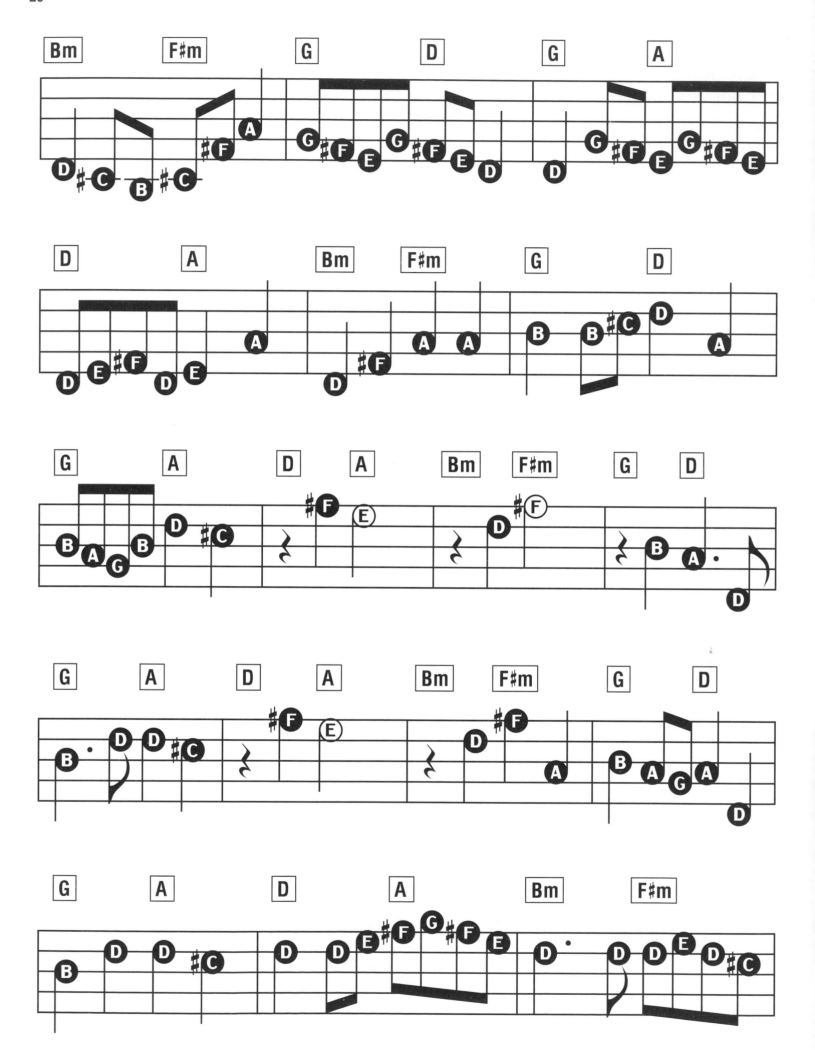

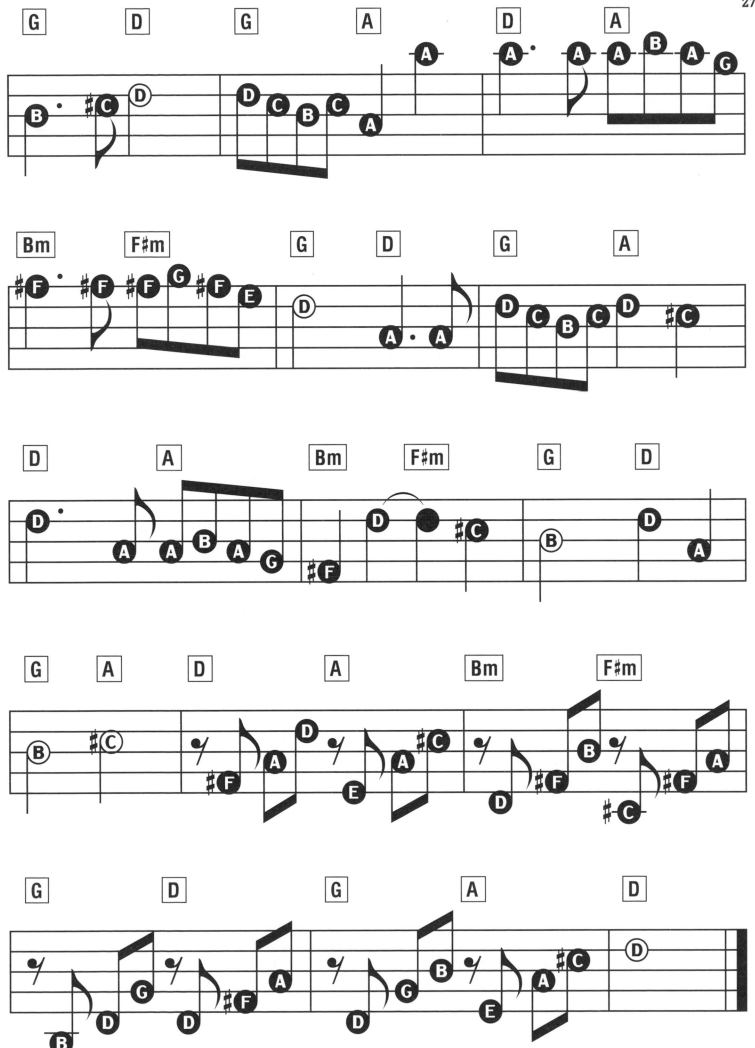

Baby Shark

Registration 2
Rhythm: Techno, 4-beat

Traditional Nursery Rhyme
Arranged by Pinkfong and KidzCastle

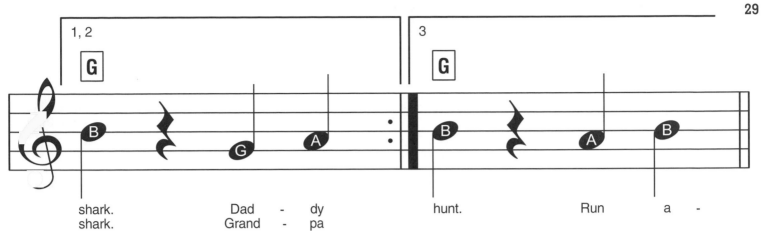

1, 2 **G** | 3 **G**

shark.   Dad - dy   hunt.   Run   a -
shark.   Grand - pa

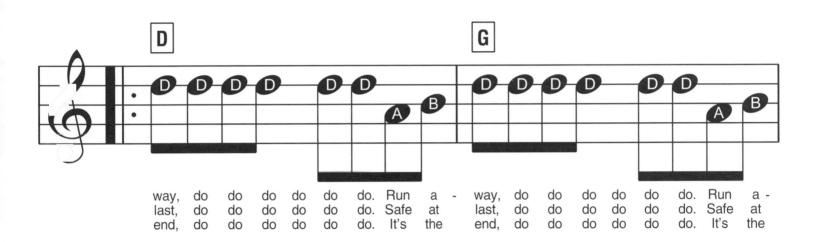

D   **G**

way, do do do do do do. Run a - way, do do do do do do. Run a -
last, do do do do do do. Safe at last, do do do do do do. Safe at
end, do do do do do do. It's the end, do do do do do do. It's the

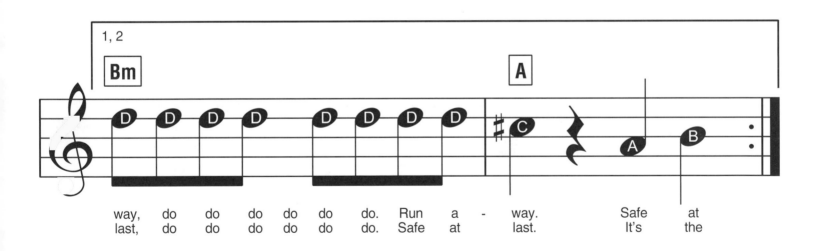

1, 2 **Bm**   **A**

way, do do do do do do. Run a - way.   Safe   at
last, do do do do do do. Safe at last.   It's   the

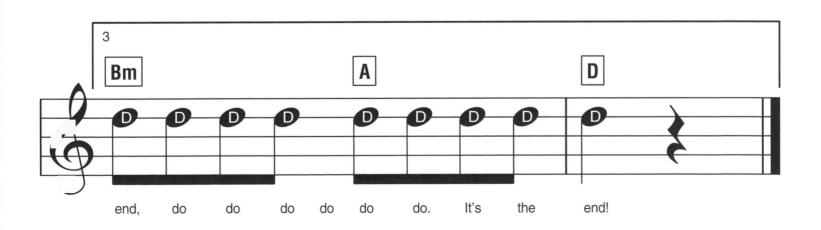

3 **Bm**   **A**   **D**

end, do do do do do do. It's the end!

Can't Help Falling in Love
from the Paramount Picture BLUE HAWAII

Registration 3
Rhythm: Ballad or Swing

Words and Music by George David Weiss,
Hugo Peretti and Luigi Creatore

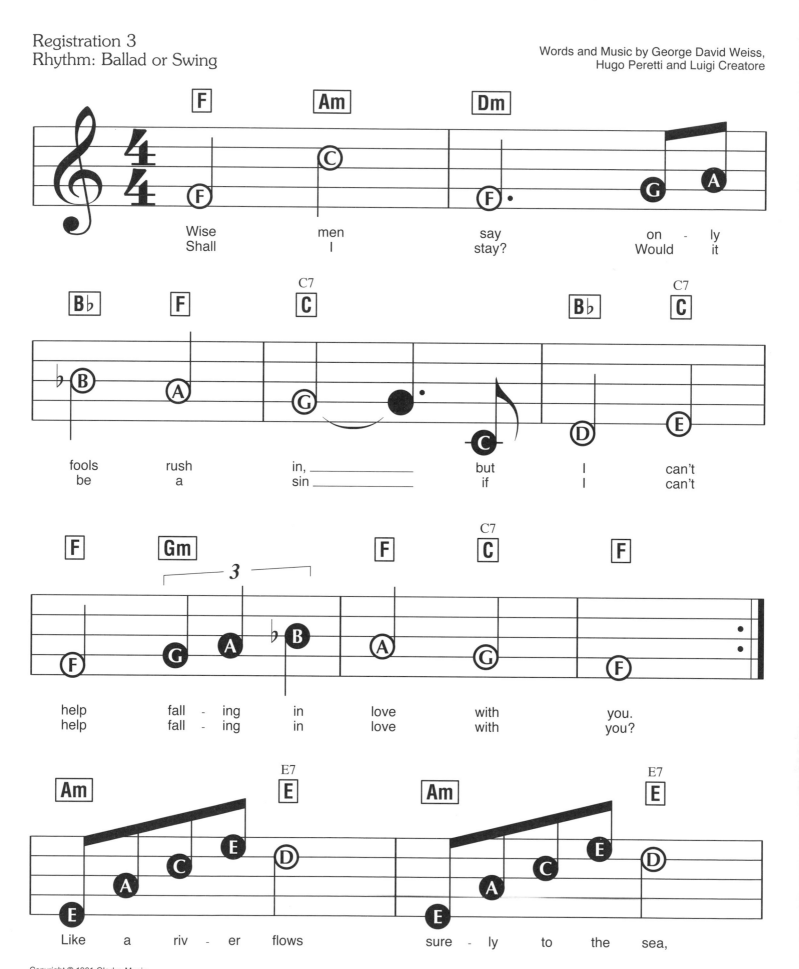

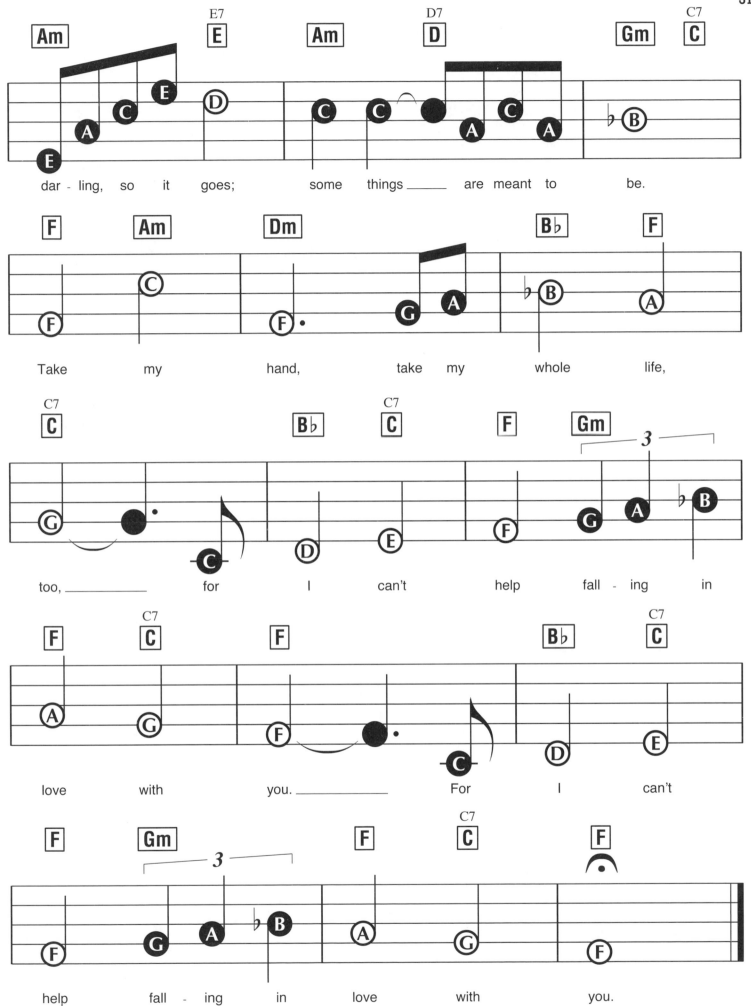

Page 31

Hallelujah

Registration 4
Rhythm: 6/8 March

Words and Music by
Leonard Cohen

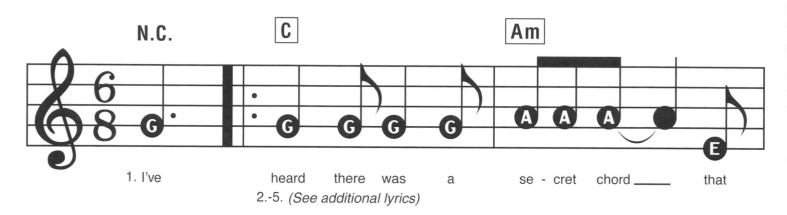

1. I've heard there was a se-cret chord _____ that
2.-5. *(See additional lyrics)*

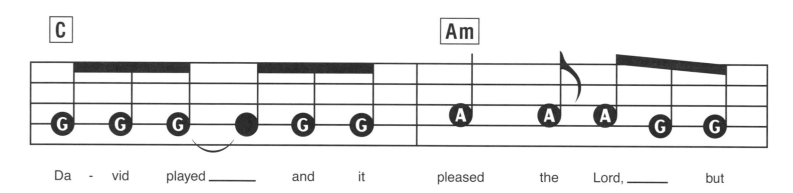

Da - vid played _____ and it pleased the Lord, _____ but

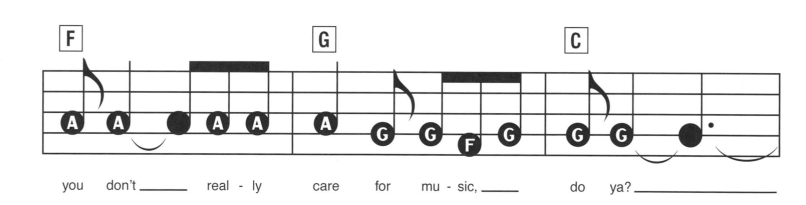

you don't _____ real - ly care for mu - sic, _____ do ya? _____

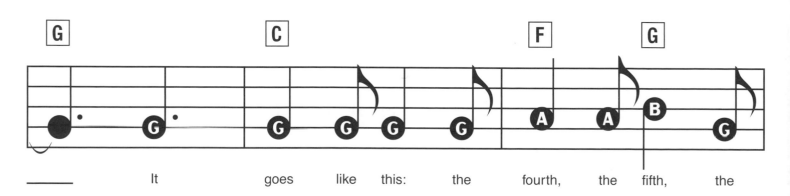

_____ It goes like this: the fourth, the fifth, the

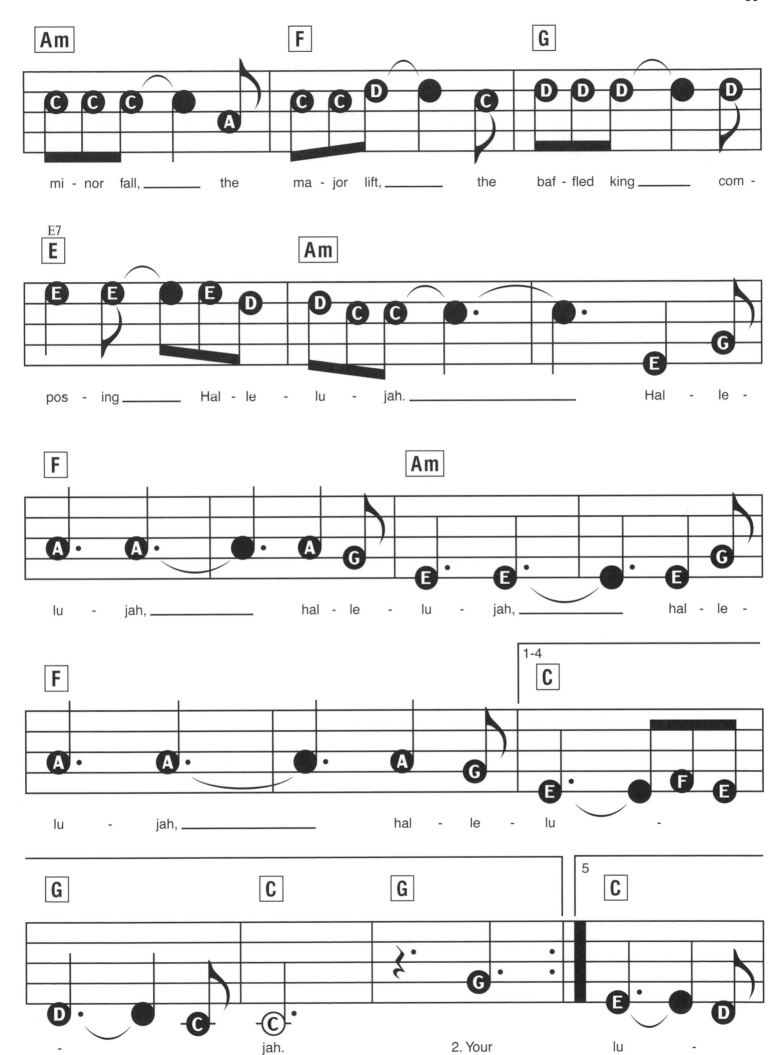

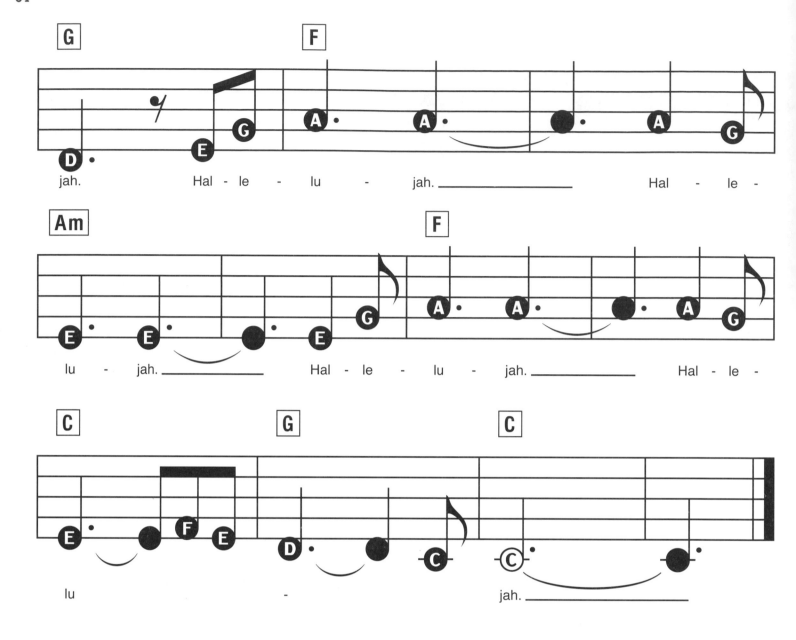

Additional Lyrics

2. Your faith was strong but you needed proof.
You saw her bathing on the roof.
Her beauty and the moonlight overthrew ya.
She tied you to a kitchen chair.
She broke your throne, she cut your hair.
And from your lips she drew the Hallelujah.

3. Maybe I have been here before.
I know this room, I've walked this floor.
I used to live alone before I knew ya.
I've seen your flag on the marble arch.
Love is not a vict'ry march.
It's a cold and it's a broken Hallelujah.

4. There was a time you let me know
What's real and going on below.
But now you never show it to me, do ya?
And remember when I moved in you.
The holy dark was movin', too,
And every breath we drew was Hallelujah.

5. Maybe there's a God above,
And all I ever learned from love
Was how to shoot at someone who outdrew ya.
And it's not a cry you can hear at night.
It's not somebody who's seen the light.
It's a cold and it's a broken Hallelujah.

Chariots of Fire
from the Feature Film CHARIOTS OF FIRE

Registration 5
Rhythm: Rock or Disco

By Vangelis

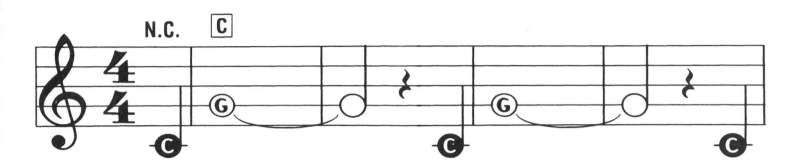

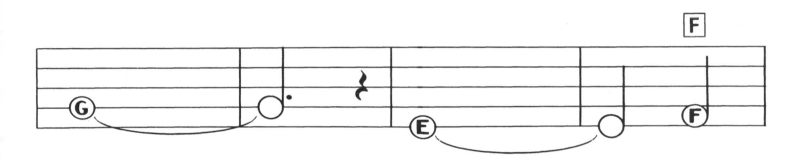

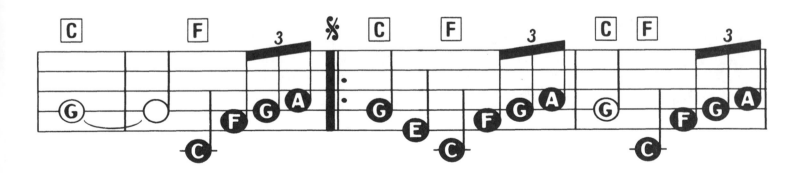

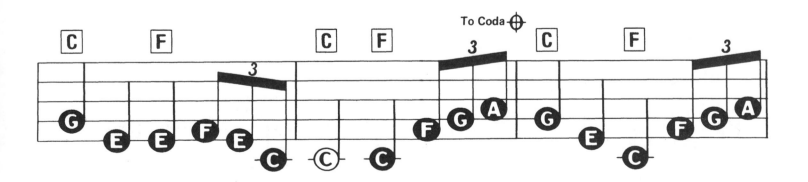

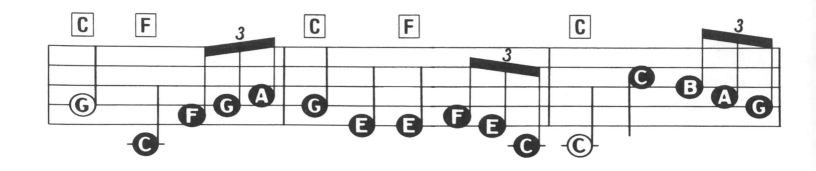

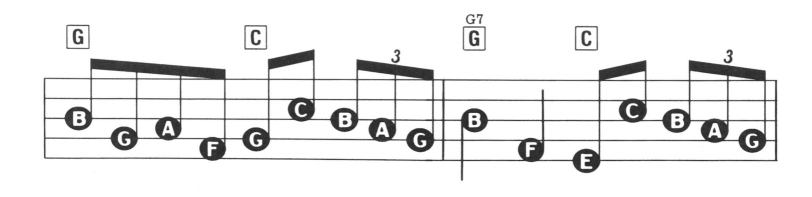

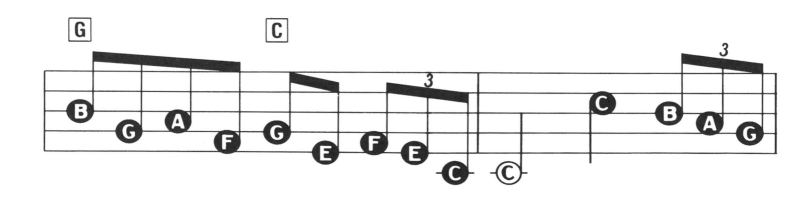

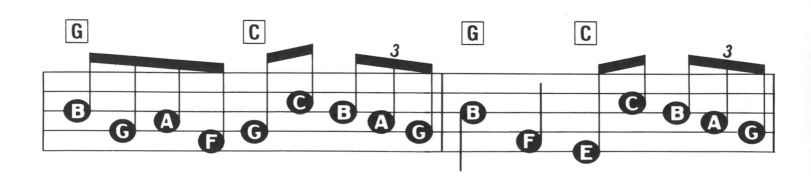

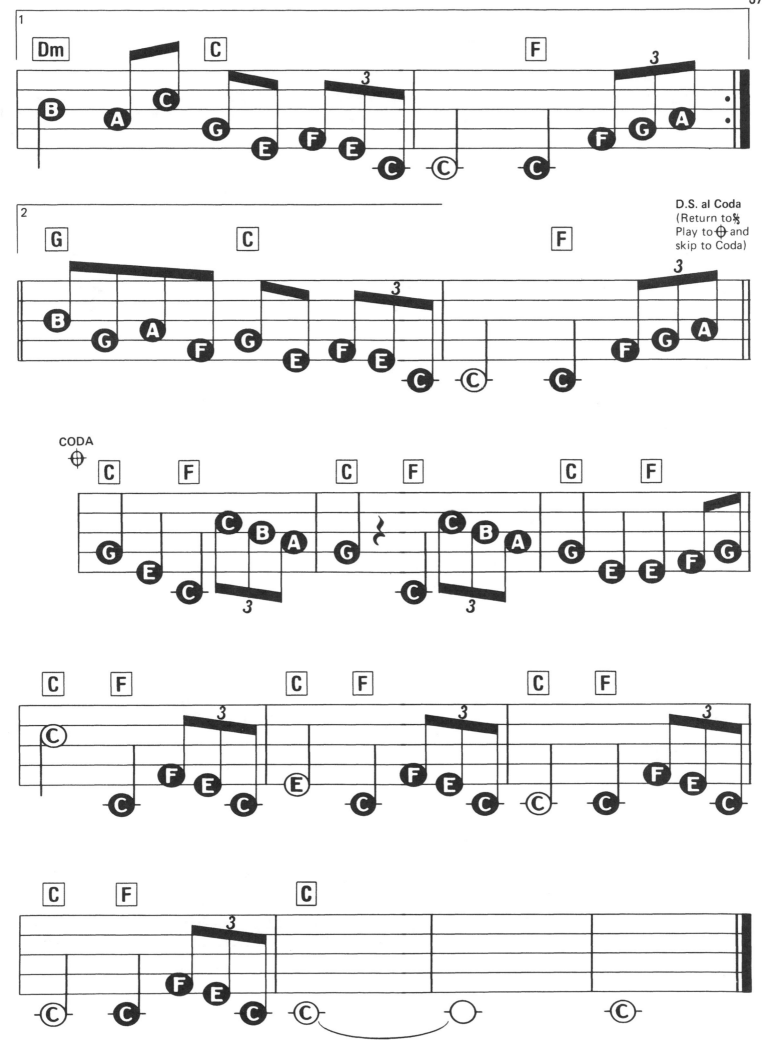

D.S. al Coda
(Return to %
Play to ⊕ and
skip to Coda)

Do-Re-Mi
from THE SOUND OF MUSIC

Registration 4
Rhythm: Fox Trot or March

Lyrics by Oscar Hammerstein II
Music by Richard Rodgers

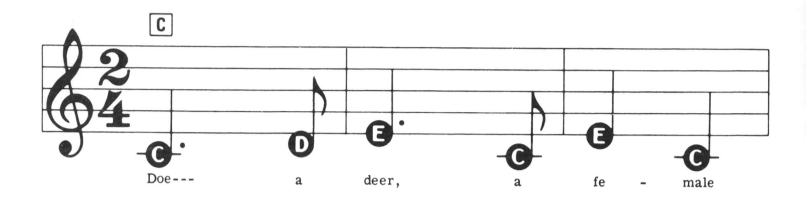

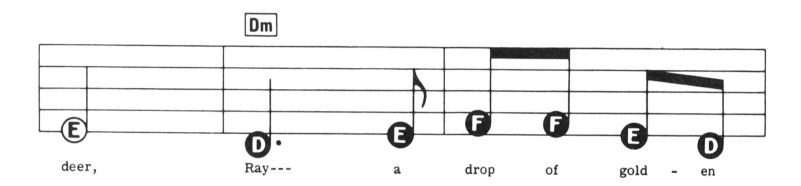

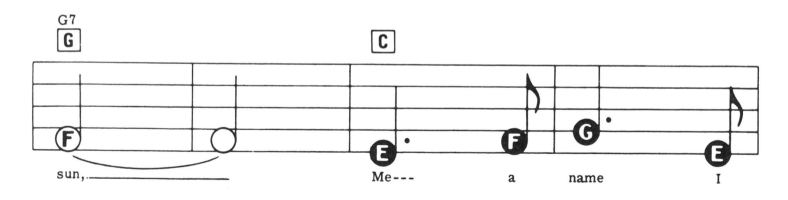

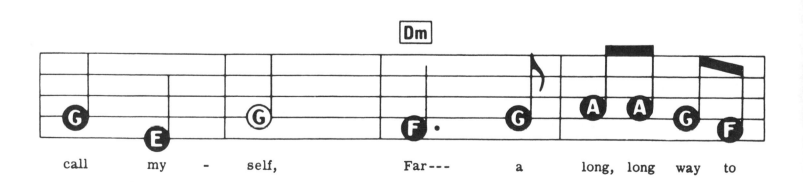

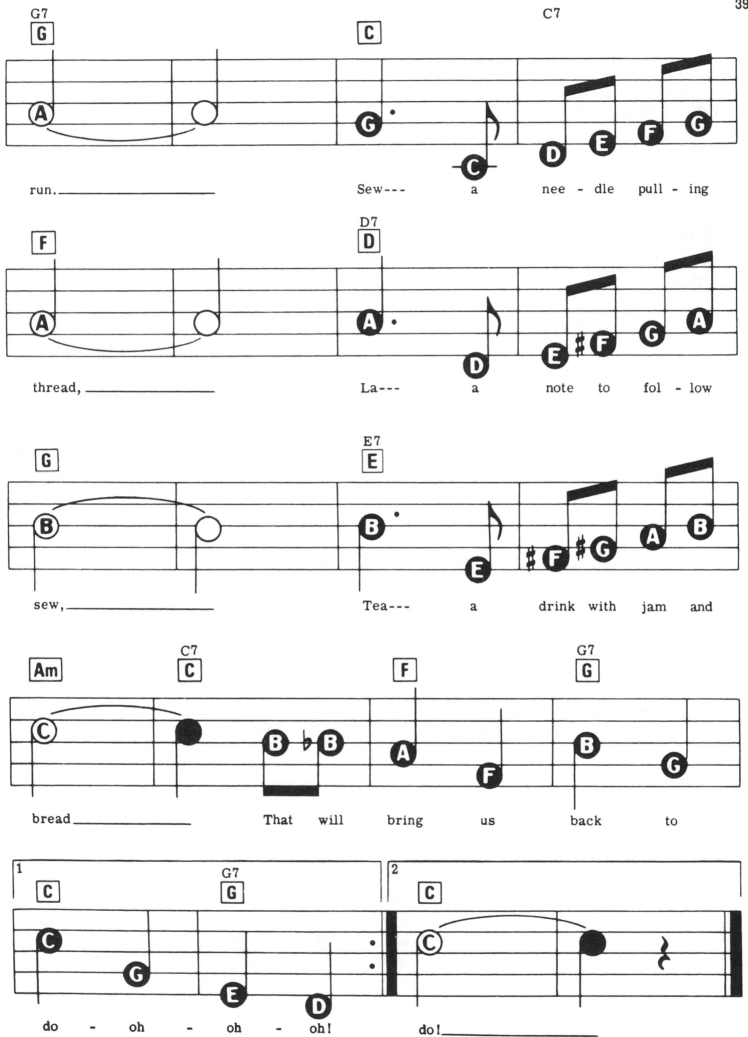

Don't Stop Believin'

Registration 1
Rhythm: 8-Beat or Rock

Words and Music by Steve Perry,
Neal Schon and Jonathan Cain

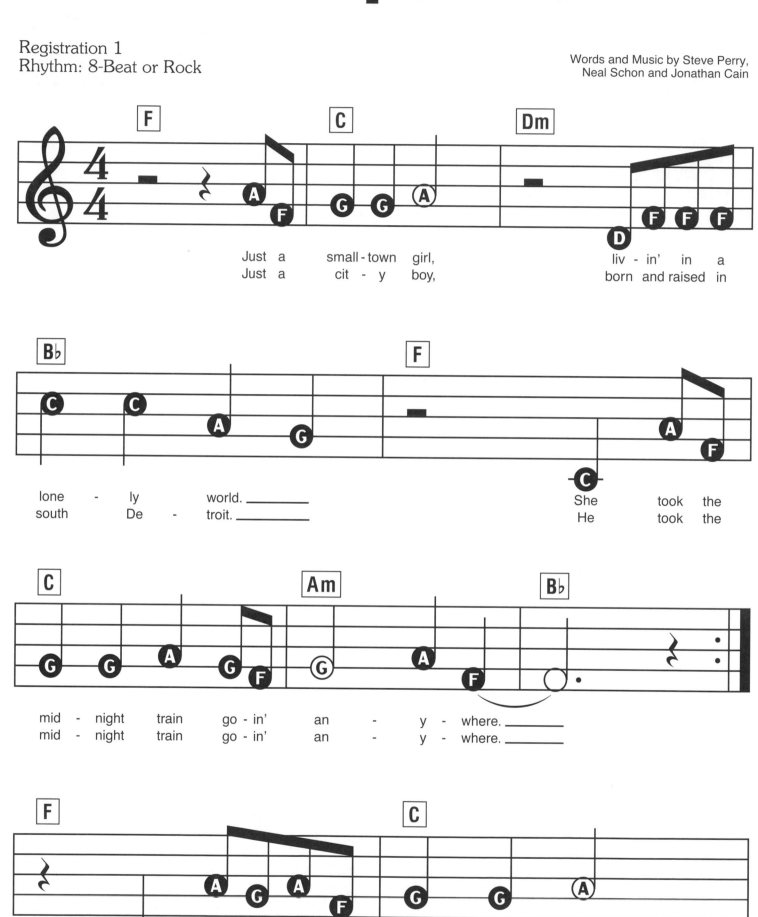

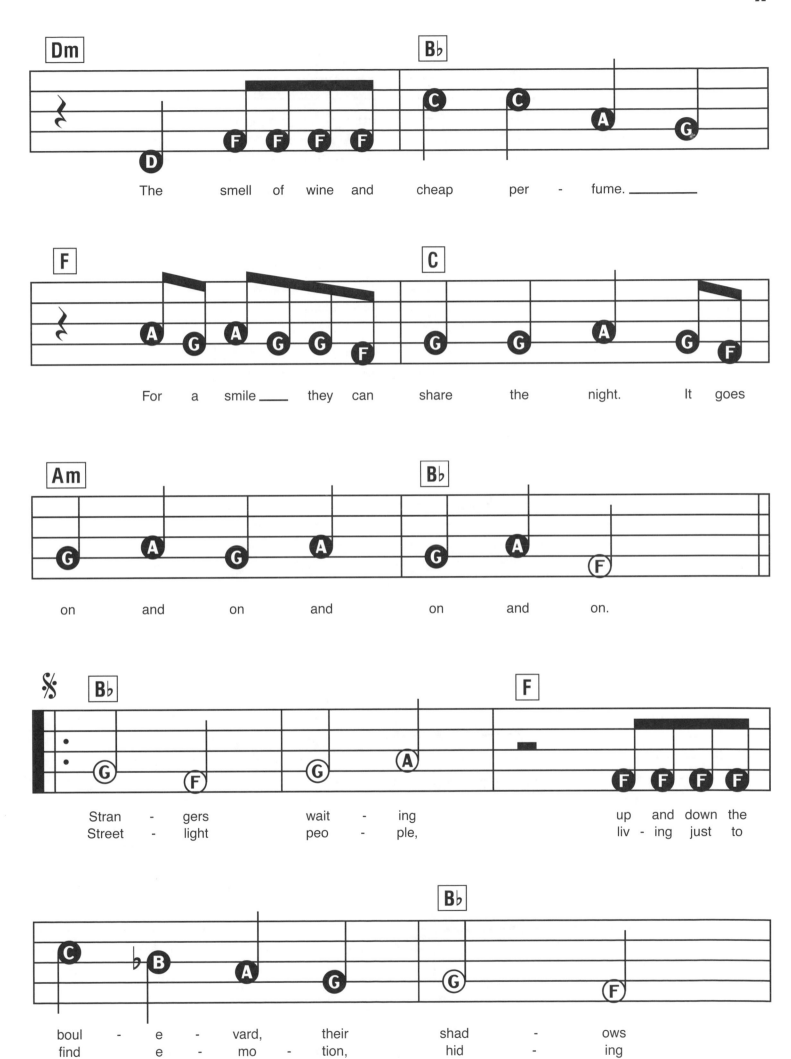

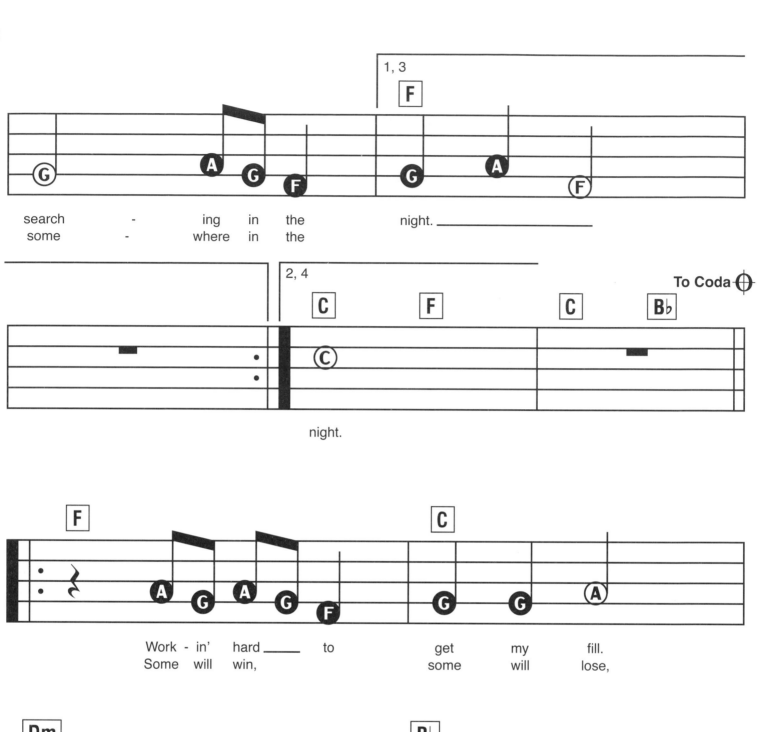

search - ing in the night.
some - where in the

night.

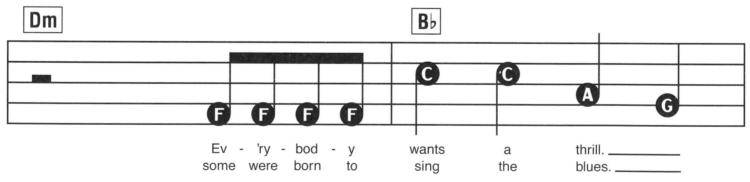

Work - in' hard _____ to get my fill.
Some will win, some will lose,

Ev - 'ry - bod - y wants a thrill. _____
some were born to sing the blues. _____

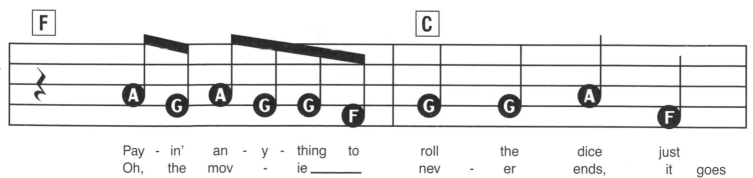

Pay - in' an - y - thing to roll the dice, just
Oh, the mov - ie _____ nev - er ends, just it goes

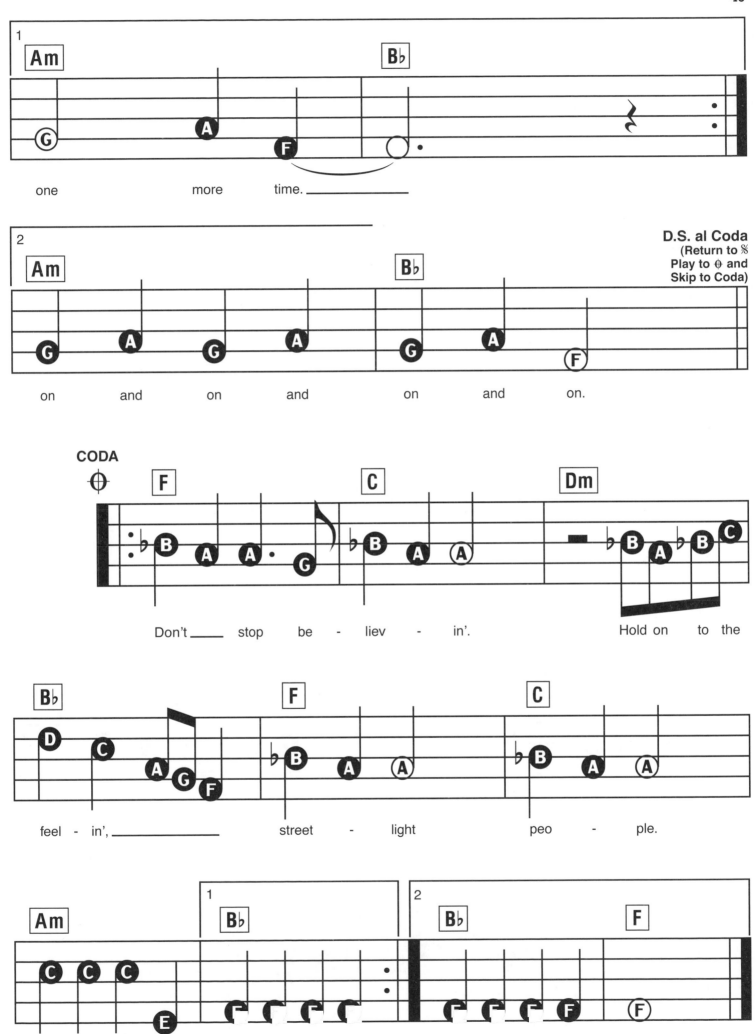

(Instrumental)

Eine kleine Nachtmusik

Registration 3
Rhythm: None

By Wolfgang Amadeus Mozart

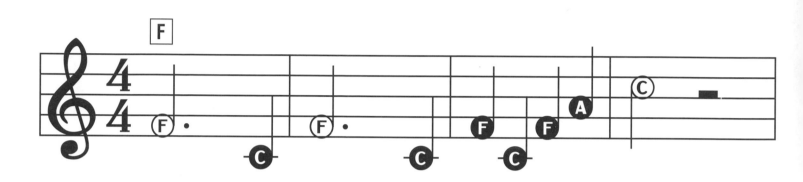

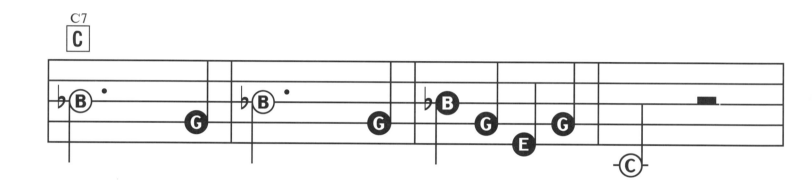

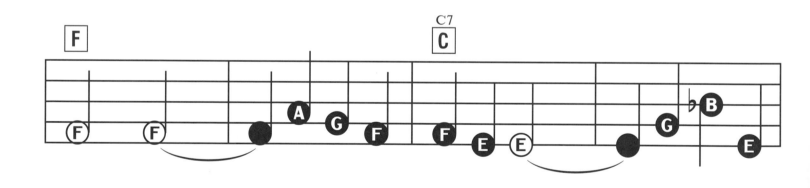

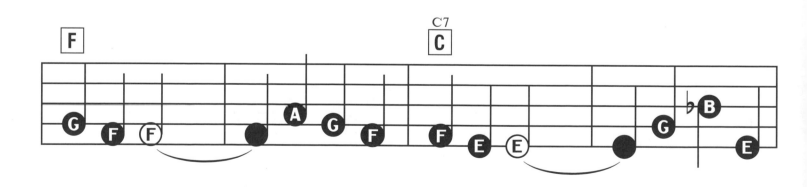

45

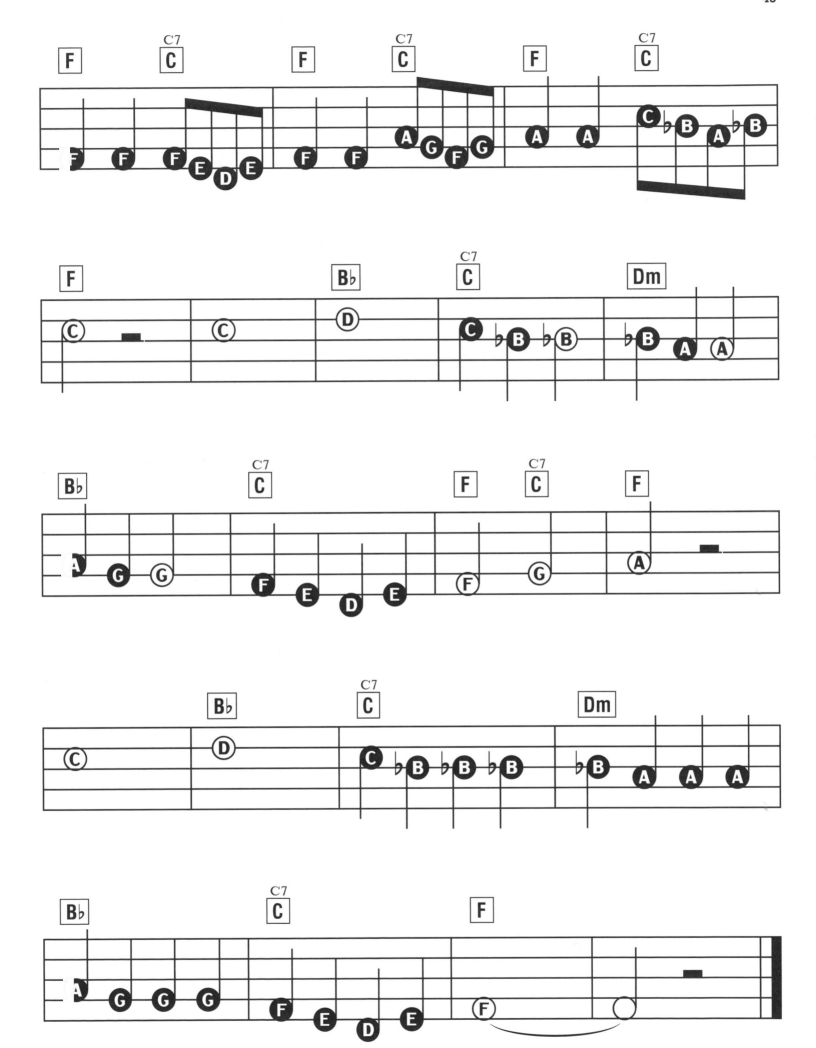

Fly Me to the Moon
(In Other Words)

Registration 2
Rhythm: Waltz or Jazz Waltz

Words and Music by
Bart Howard

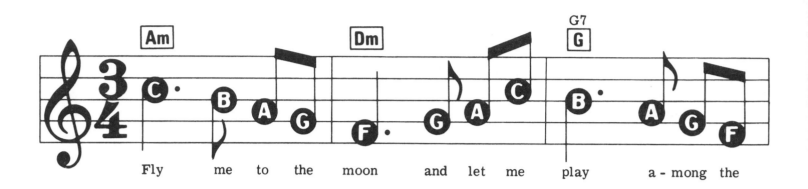

Fly me to the moon and let me play a - mong the

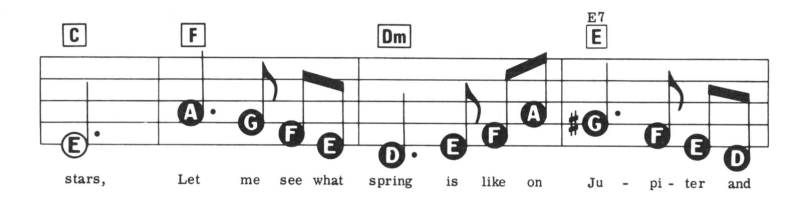

stars, Let me see what spring is like on Ju - pi - ter and

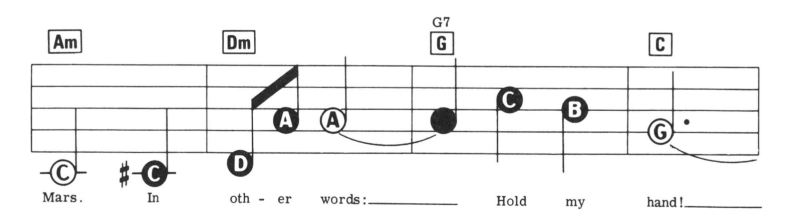

Mars. In oth - er words:_____ Hold my hand!_____

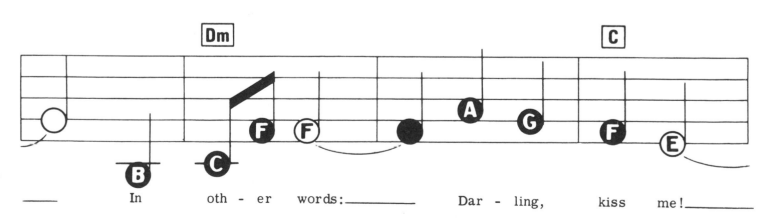

_____ In oth - er words:_____ Dar - ling, kiss me!_____

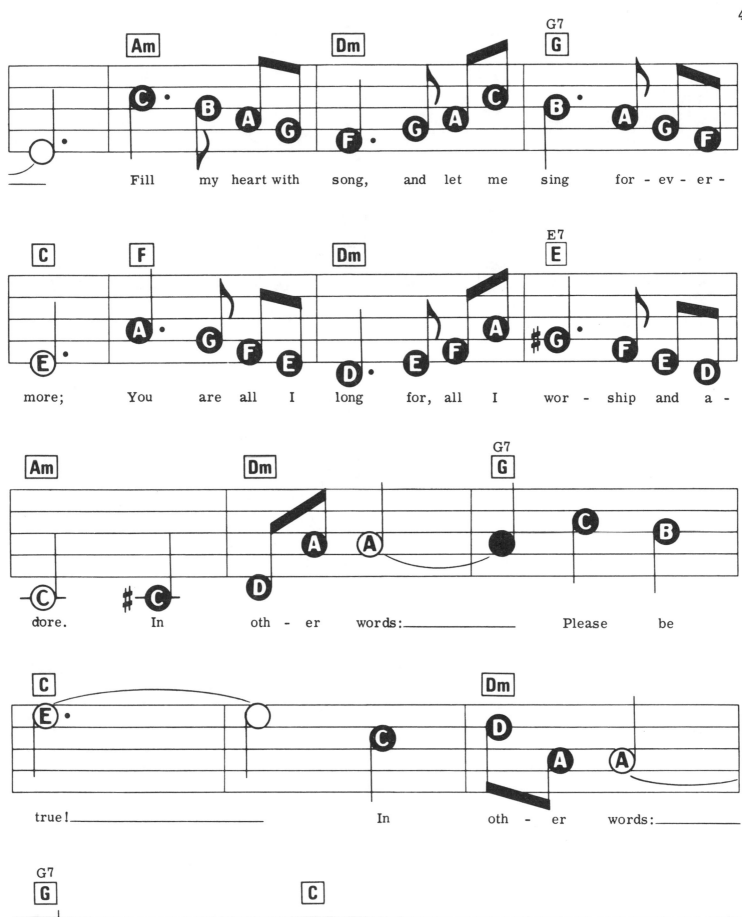

Fill my heart with song, and let me sing for - ev - er - more; You are all I long for, all I wor - ship and a - dore. In oth - er words:_____ Please be true!_____ In oth - er words:_____ I love you._____

Für Elise

Registration 8
Rhythm: Waltz or None

By Ludwig van Beethoven

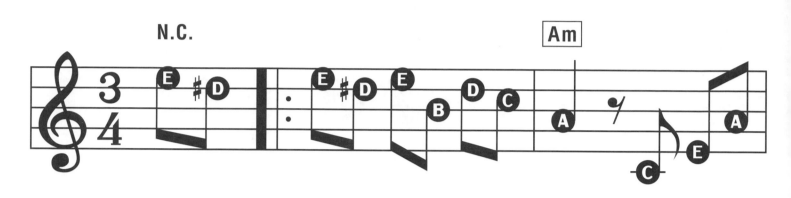

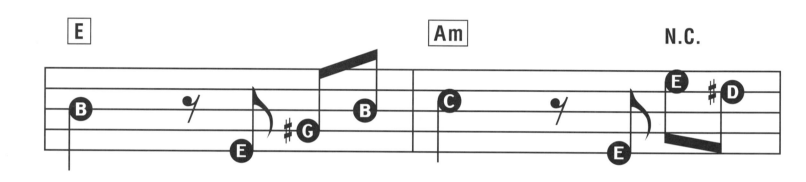

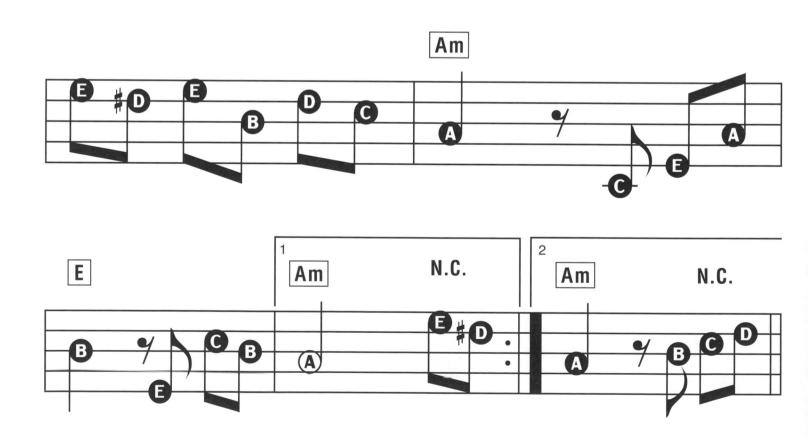

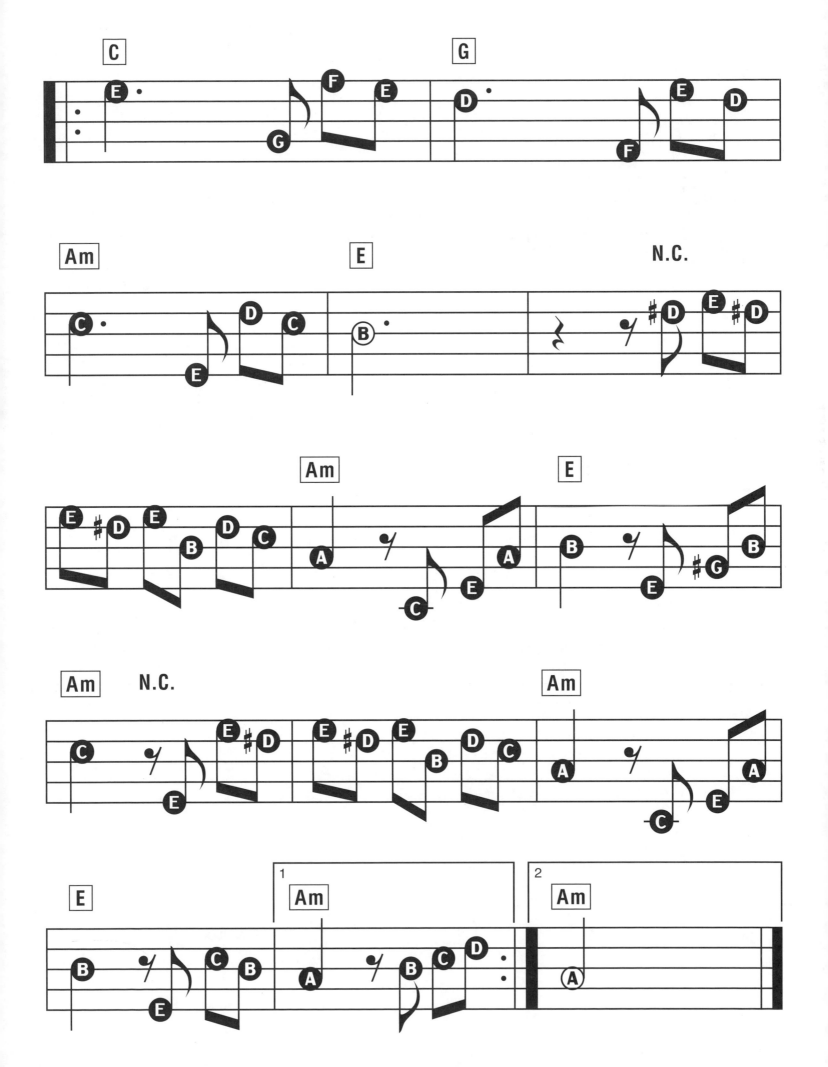

Gabriel's Oboe
from the Motion Picture THE MISSION

Registration 3
Rhythm: 4/4 Ballad

Music by Ennio Morricone

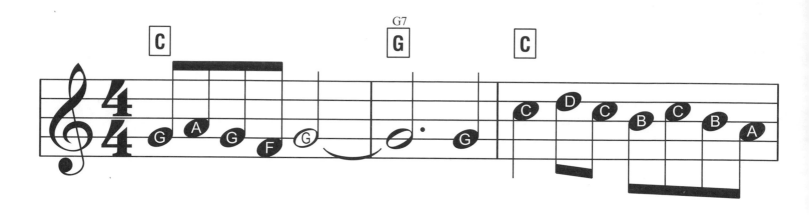

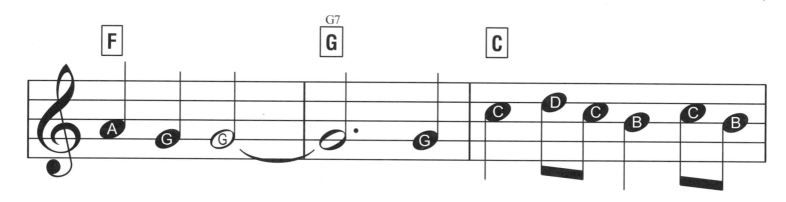

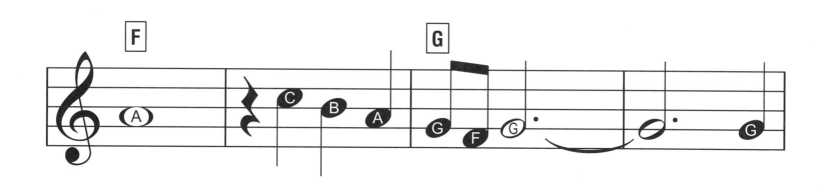

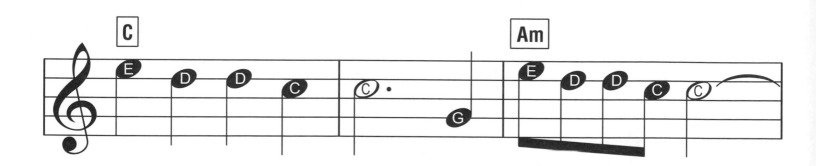

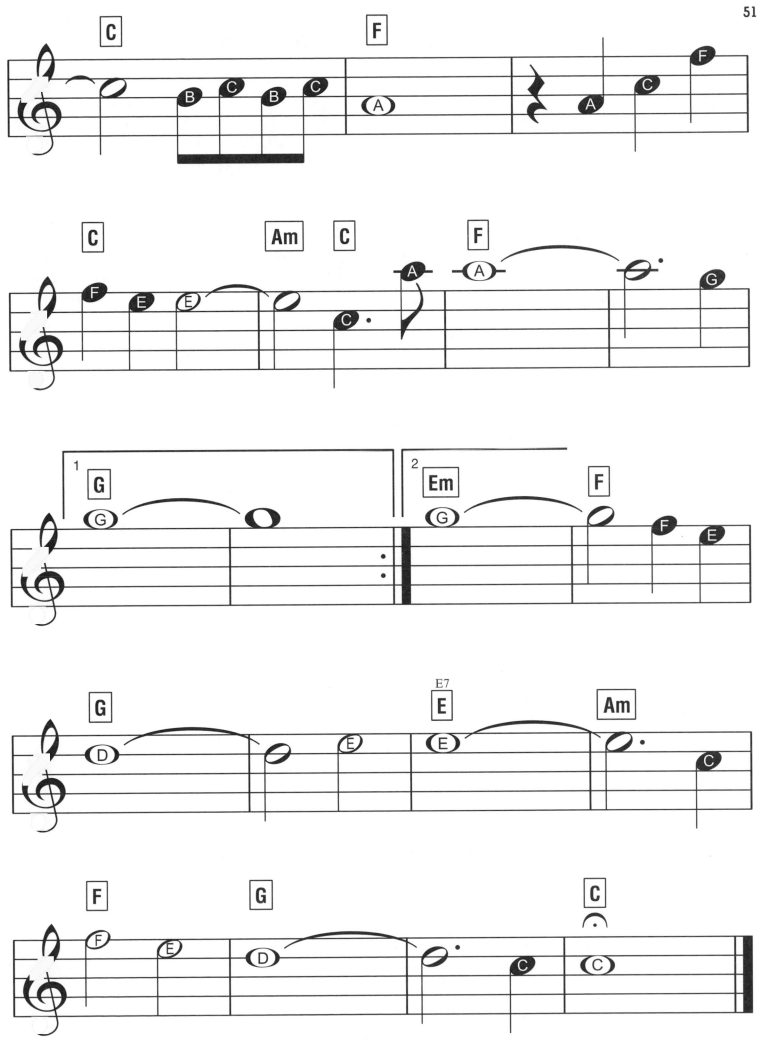

Happy Birthday to You

Registration 8
Rhythm: Waltz or None

Words and Music by Mildred J. Hill
and Patty S. Hill

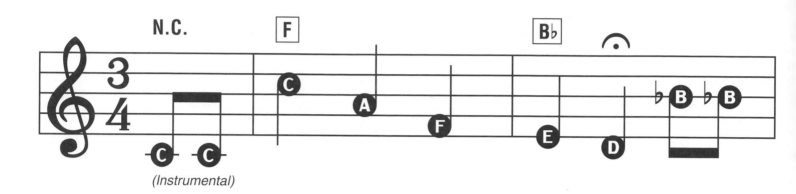

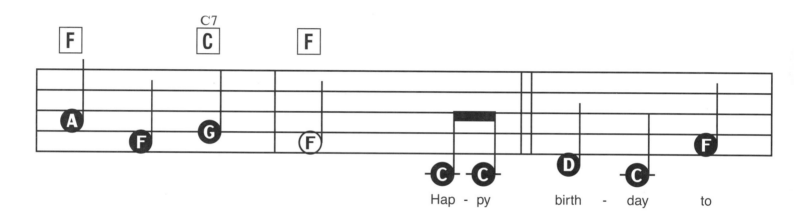

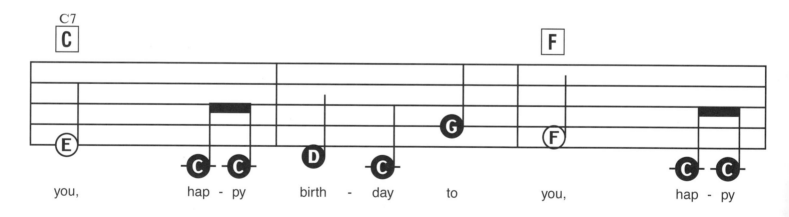

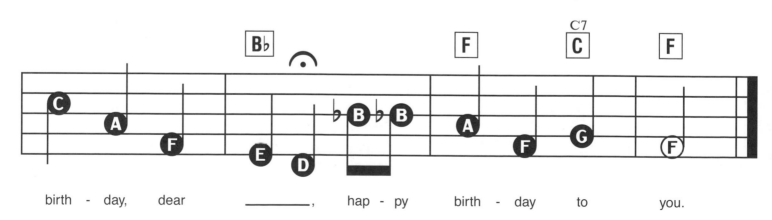

Heart and Soul
from the Paramount Short Subject A SONG IS BORN

Registration 8
Rhythm: Swing

Words by Frank Loesser
Music by Hoagy Carmichael

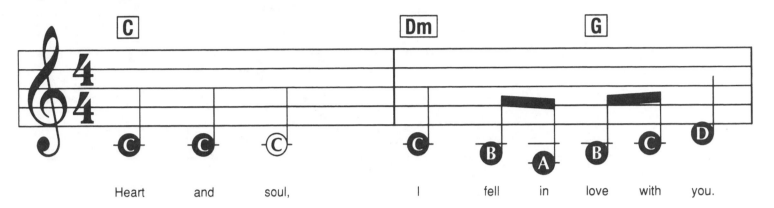

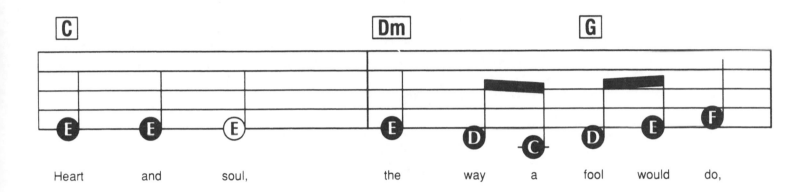

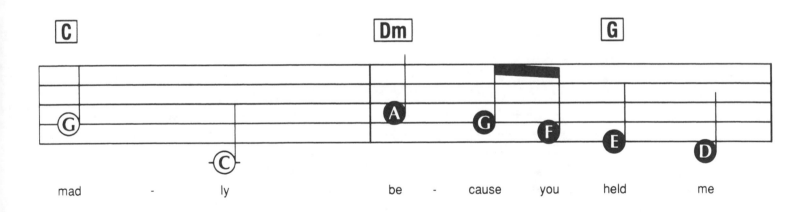

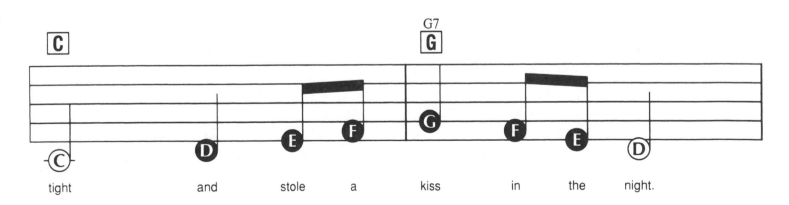

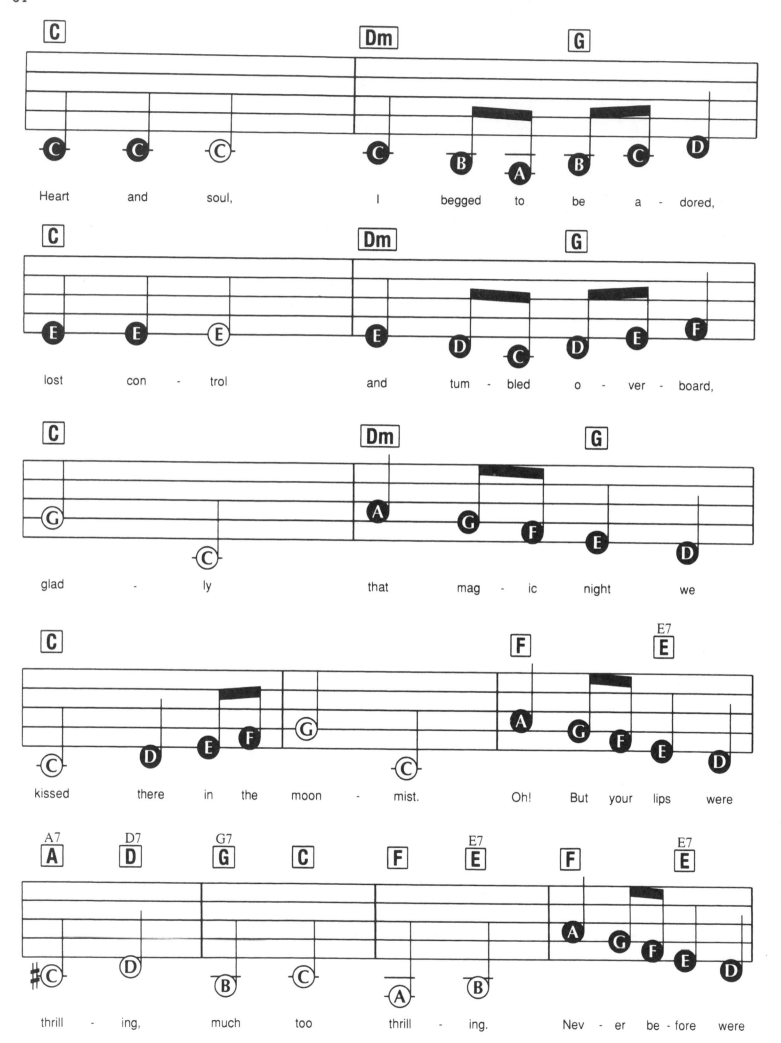

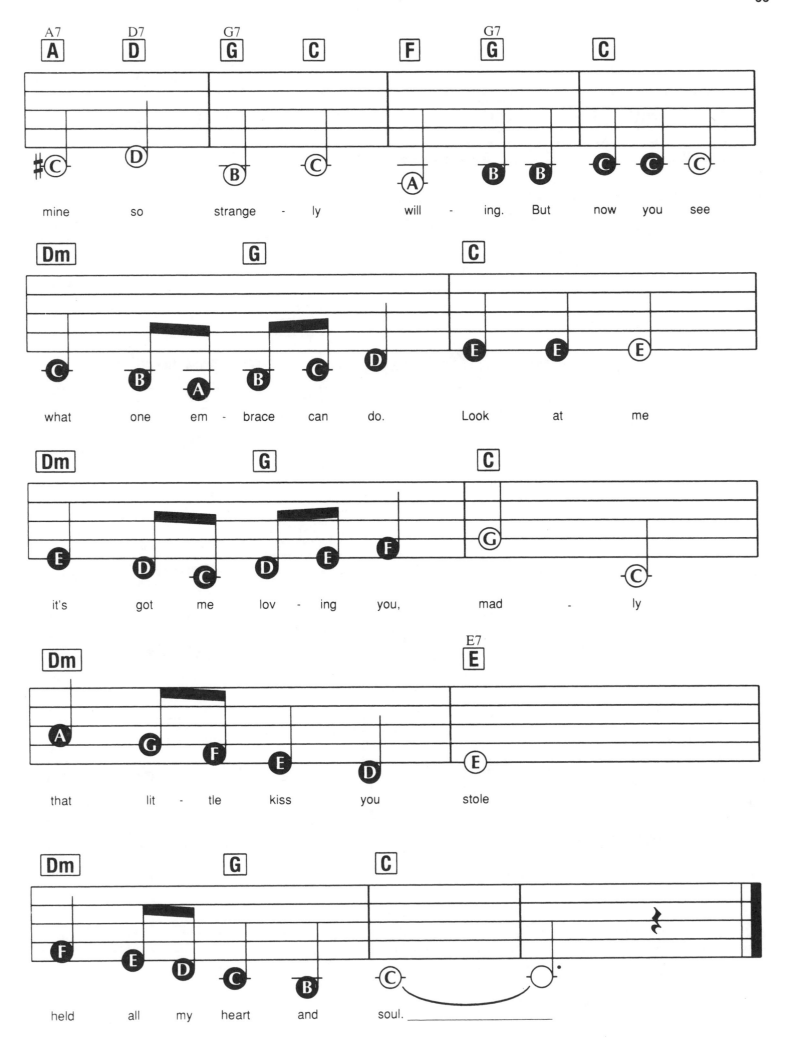

Havana

Registration 5
Rhythm: Latin or Pop

Words and Music by Camila Cabello, Louis Bell,
Pharrell Williams, Adam Feeney, Ali Tamposi,
Jeffery Lamar Williams, Brian Lee, Andrew Wotman,
Brittany Hazzard and Kaan Gunesberk

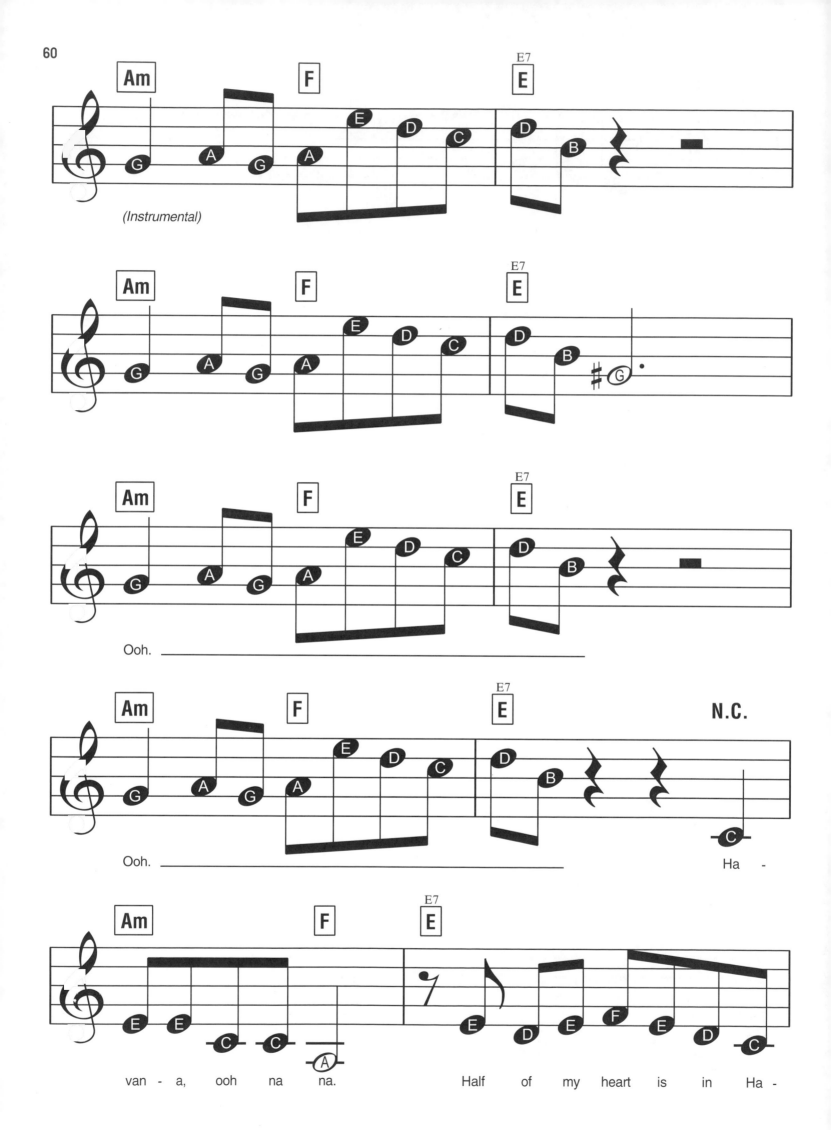

How Far I'll Go
from MOANA

Registration 1
Rhythm: Pop or Techno

Music and Lyrics by
Lin-Manuel Miranda

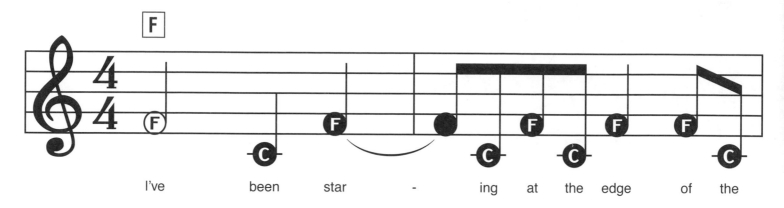

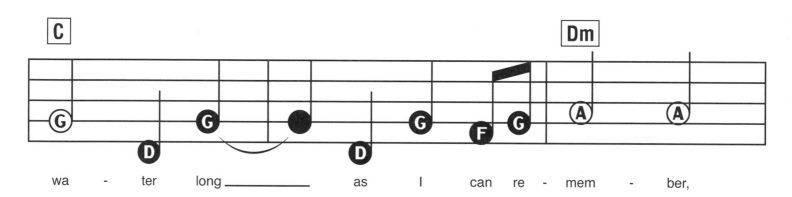

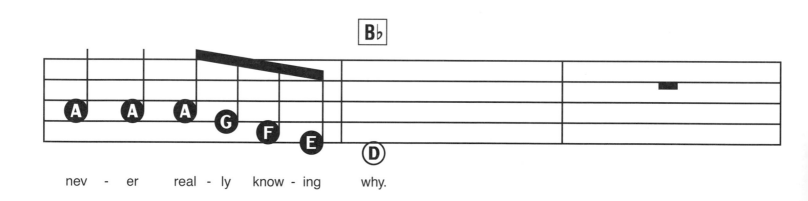

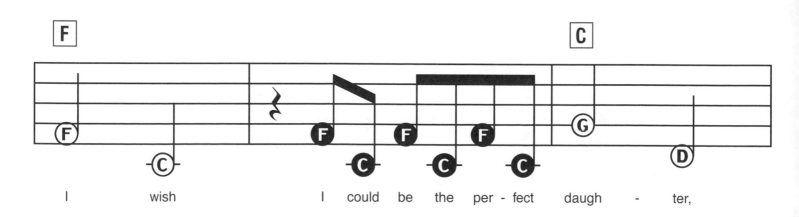

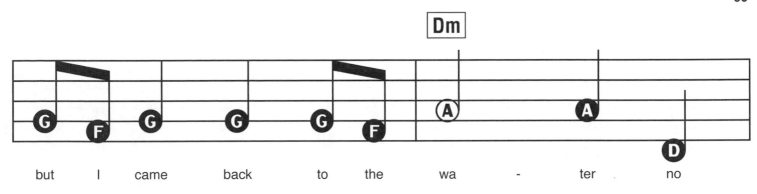

but I came back to the wa - ter no

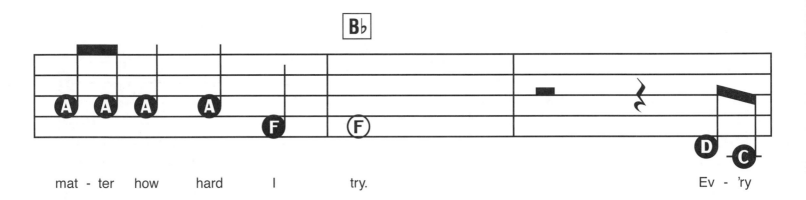

mat - ter how hard I try. Ev - 'ry

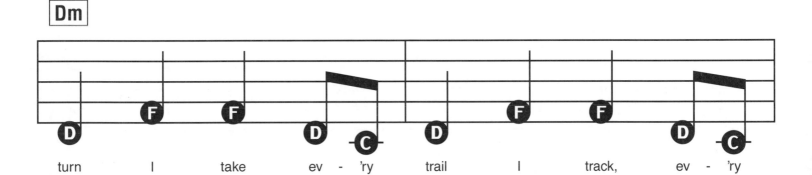

turn I take ev - 'ry trail I track, ev - 'ry

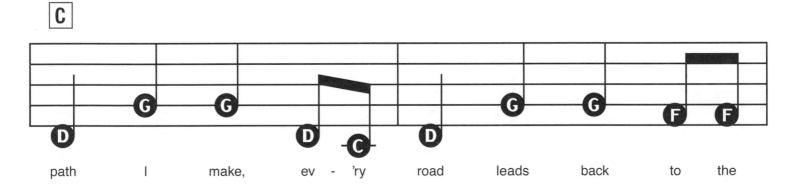

path I make, ev - 'ry road leads back to the

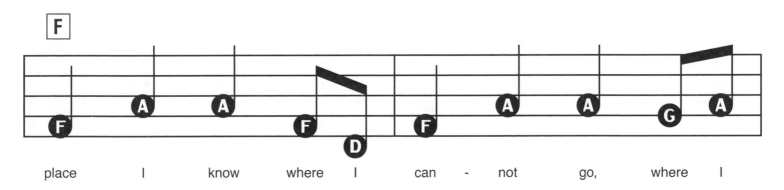

place I know where I can - not go, where I

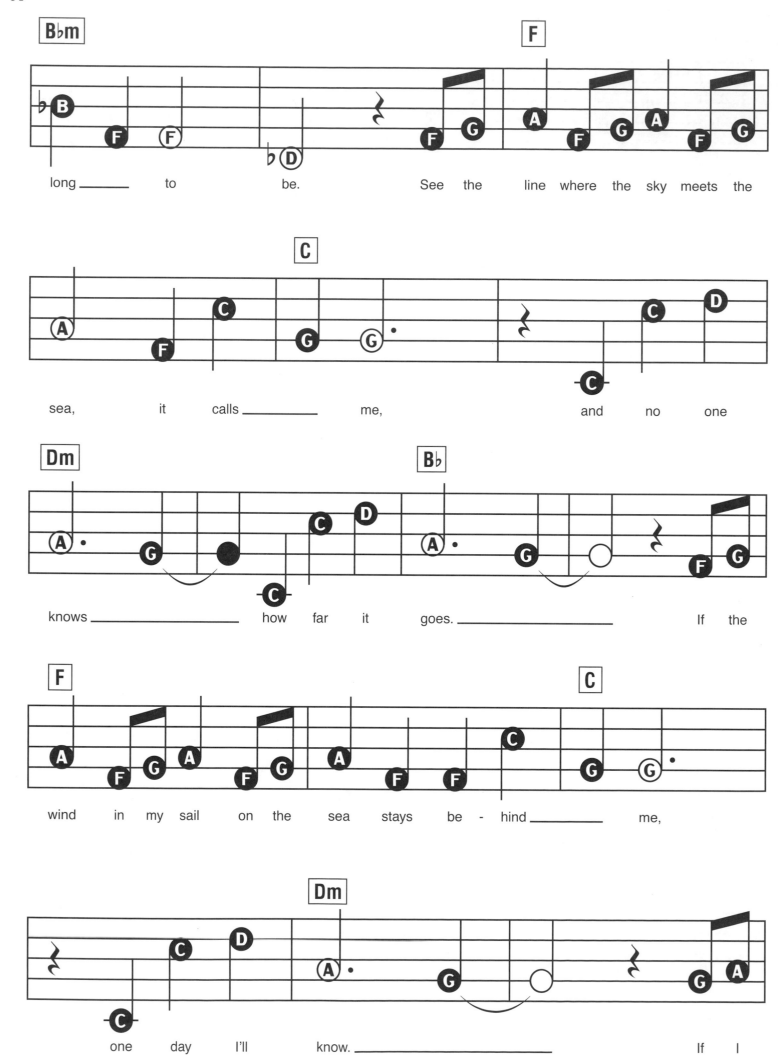

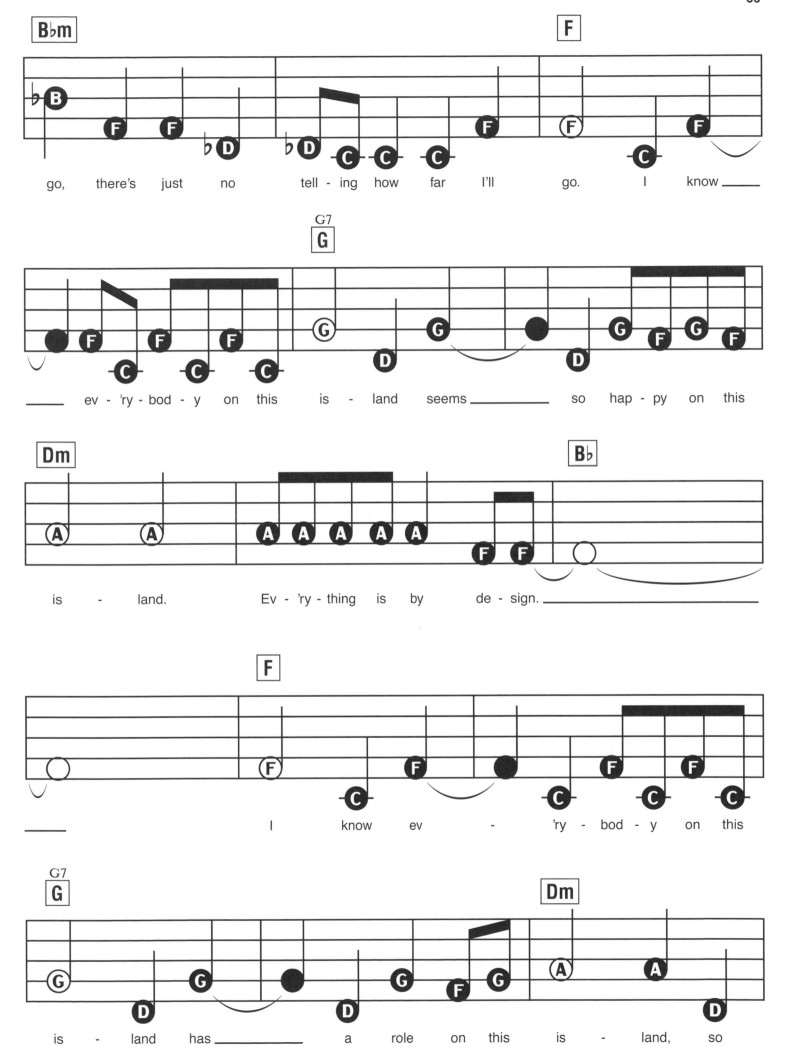

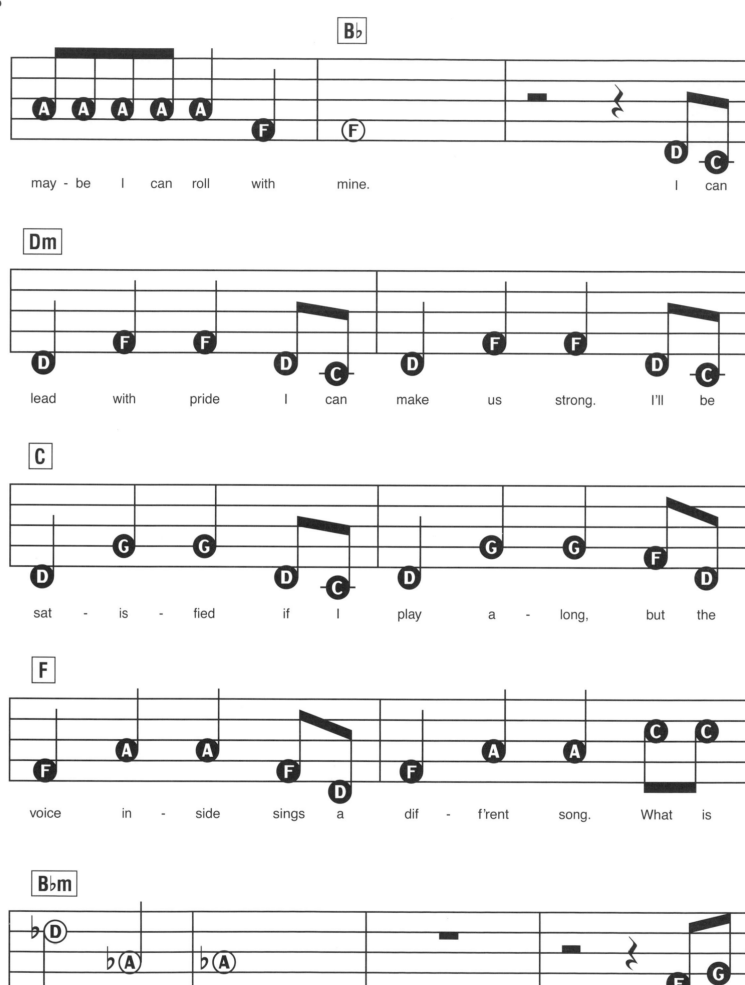

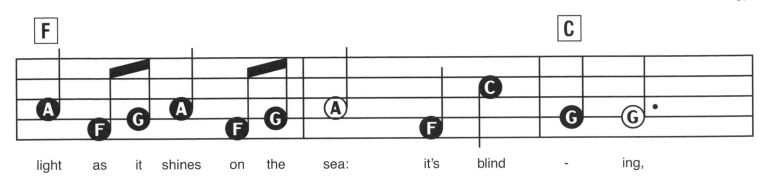

light as it shines on the sea: it's blind - ing,

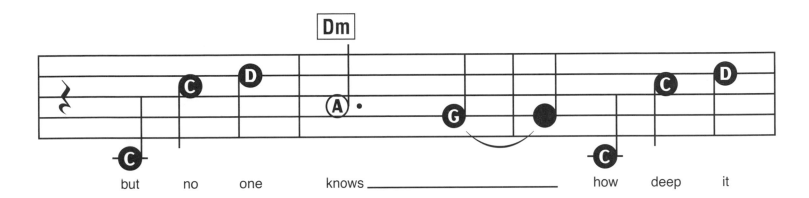

but no one knows _____ how deep it

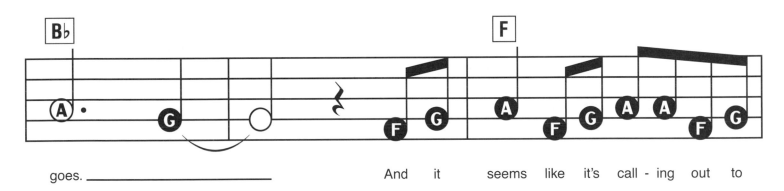

goes. _____ And it seems like it's call - ing out to

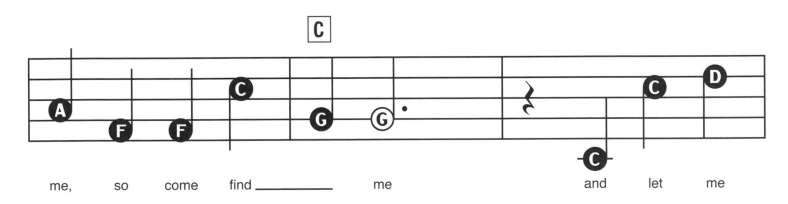

me, so come find _____ me and let me

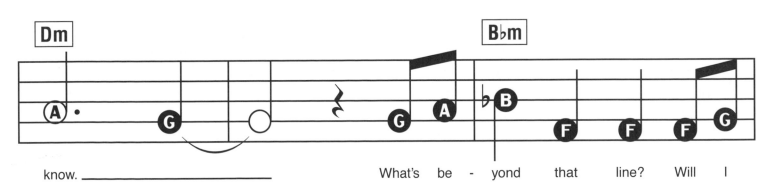

know. _____ What's be - yond that line? Will I

68

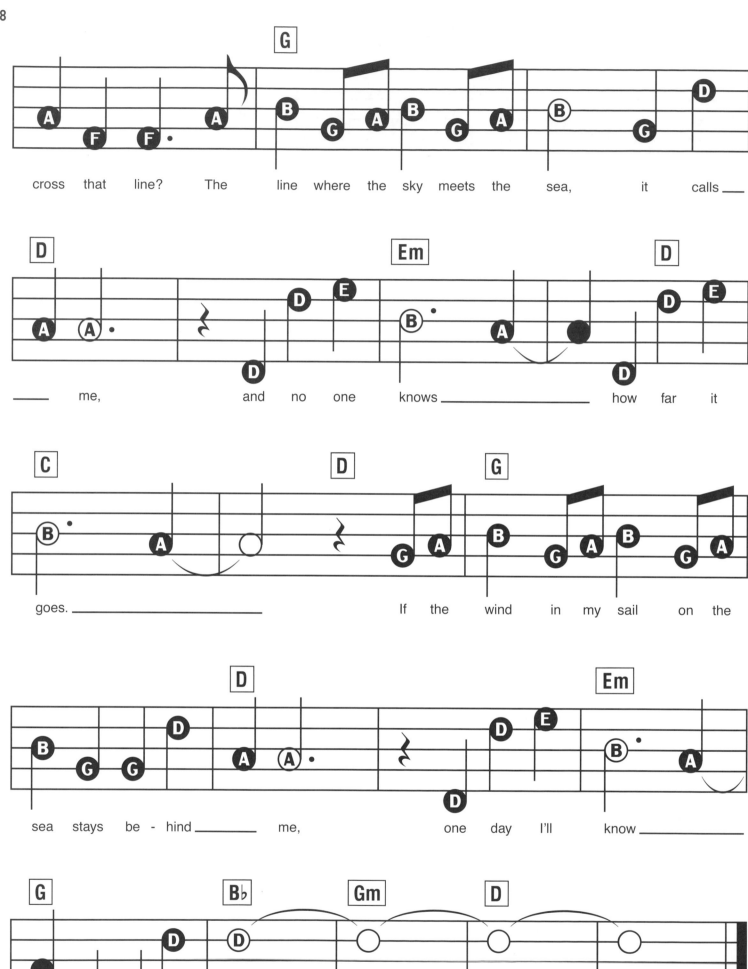

Hotel California

Registration 9
Rhythm: Rock or Disco

Words and Music by Don Henley,
Glenn Frey and Don Felder

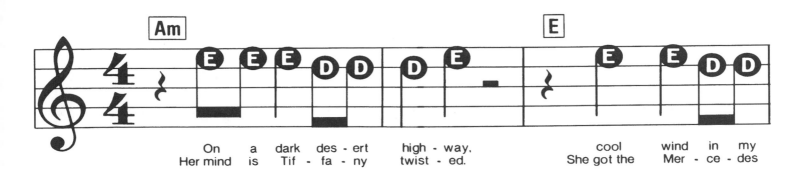

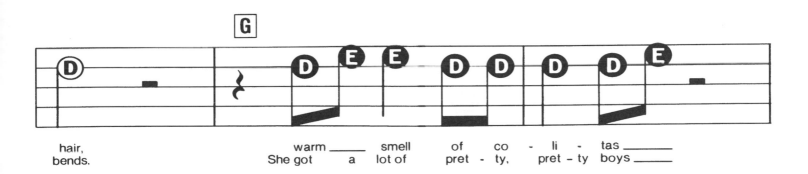

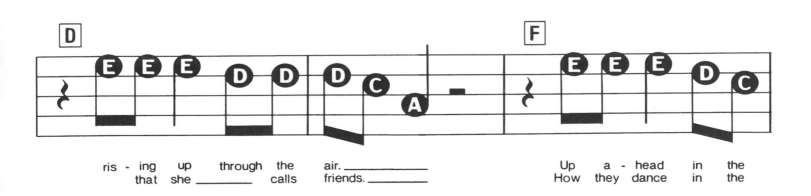

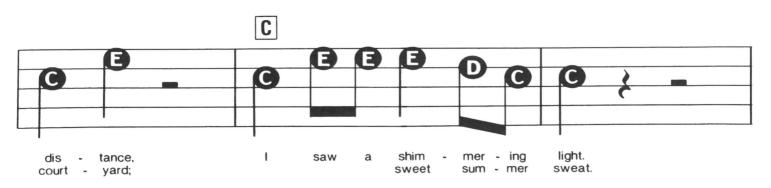

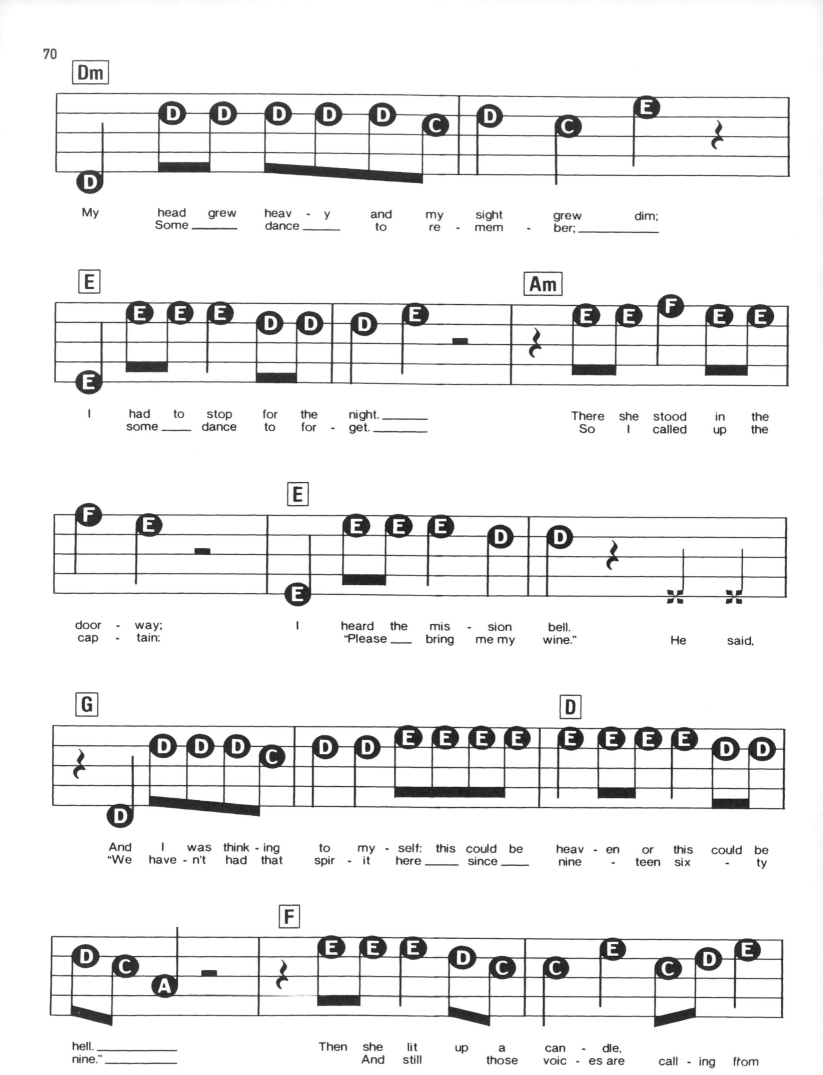

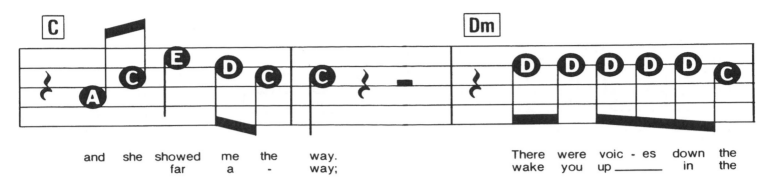

and she showed me the way.
far a - way;

There were voic - es down the
wake you up _____ in the

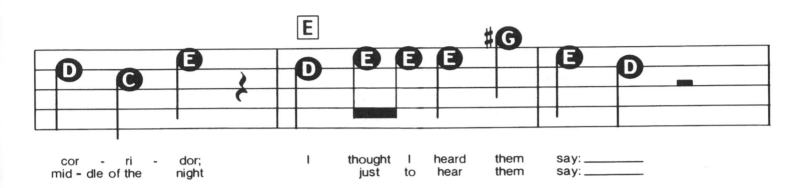

cor - ri - dor;
mid - dle of the night

I thought I heard them say: _____
just to hear them say: _____

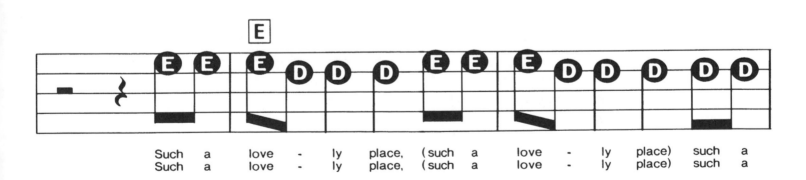

"Wel - come to the Ho - tel Cal - i - for - nia.
"Wel - come to the Ho - tel Cal - i - for - nia.

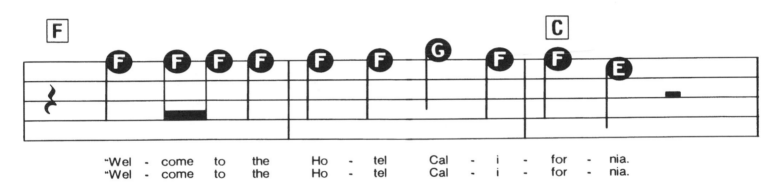

Such a love - ly place, (such a love - ly place) such a
Such a love - ly place, (such a love - ly place) such a

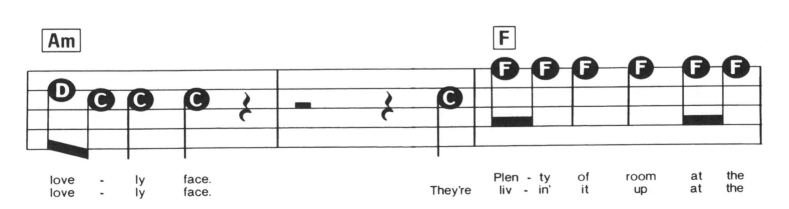

love - ly face.
love - ly face.

They're liv - in' it
Plen - ty of room at the
up at the

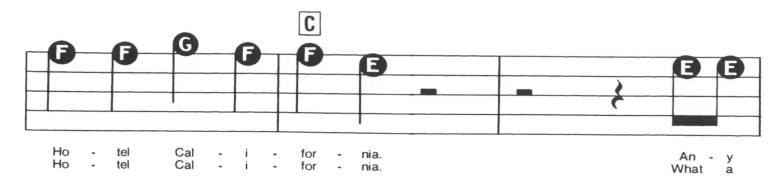

Ho - tel Cal - i - for - nia.   An - y
Ho - tel Cal - i - for - nia.   What a

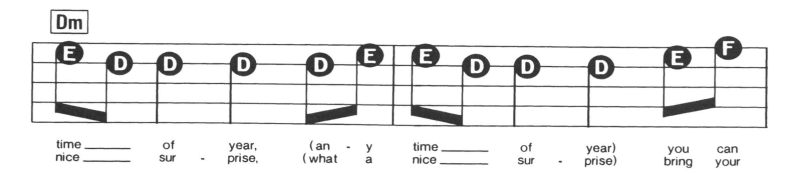

time _____ of year, (an - y time _____ of year) you can
nice _____ sur - prise, (what a nice _____ sur - prise) you bring your

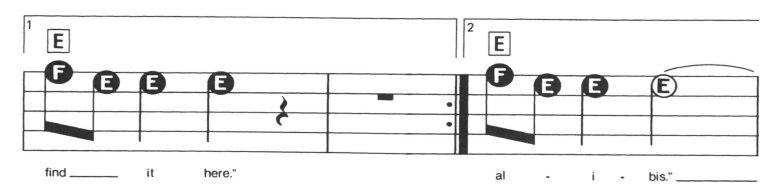

find _____ it here."   al - i - bis." _____

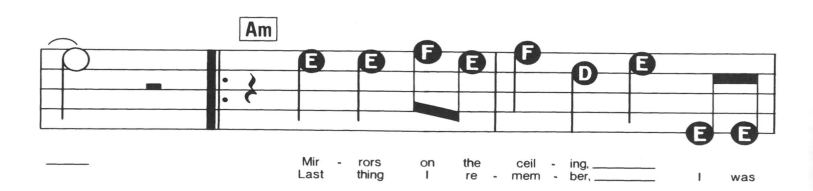

_____   Mir - rors on the ceil - ing, _____
           Last thing I re - mem - ber, _____ I was

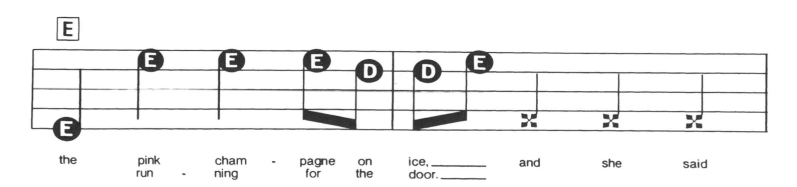

the pink cham - pagne on ice, _____ and she said
run - ning for the door. _____

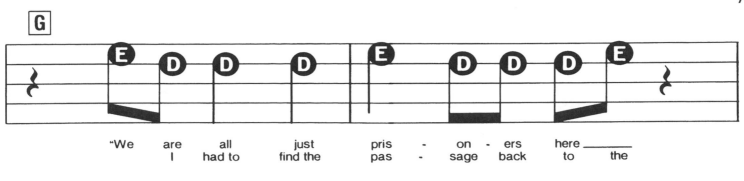

"We are all just pris - on - ers here _____
I had to just find the pas - sage back to the

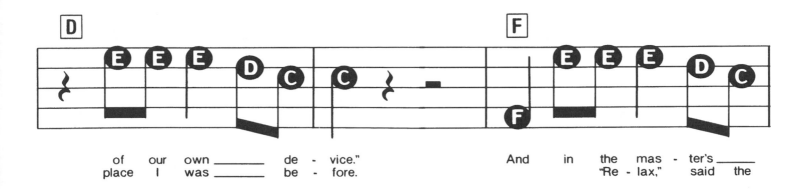

of our own _____ de - vice."
place I was _____ be - fore.

And in the mas - ter's _____
"Re - lax," said the

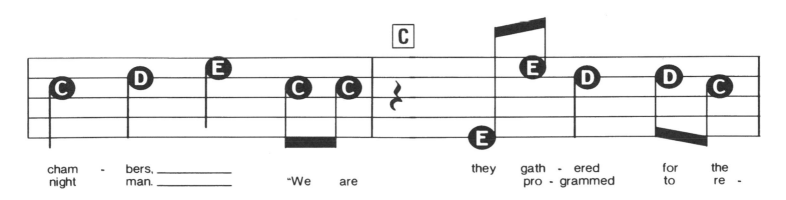

cham - bers, _____
night man. _____ "We are

they gath - ered for the
pro - grammed to re -

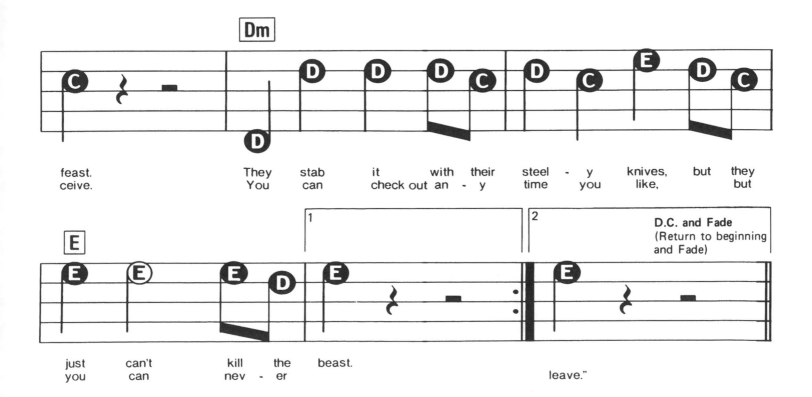

feast.
ceive.

They stab it with their steel - y knives, but they
You can check out an - y time you like, but

1

just can't kill the beast.

2

D.C. and Fade
(Return to beginning
and Fade)

you can nev - er   leave."

I Want It That Way

Registration 4
Rhythm: 8-Beat or Rock

Words and Music by Max Martin
and Andreas Carlsson

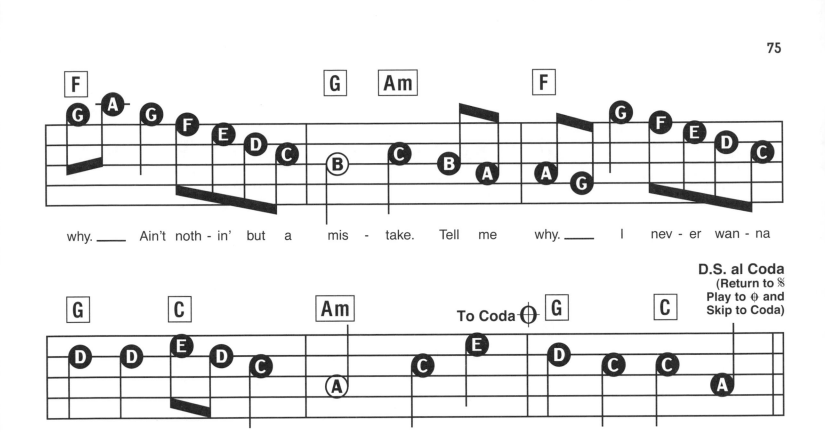

why. ____ Ain't noth - in' but a mis - take. Tell me why. ____ I nev - er wan - na

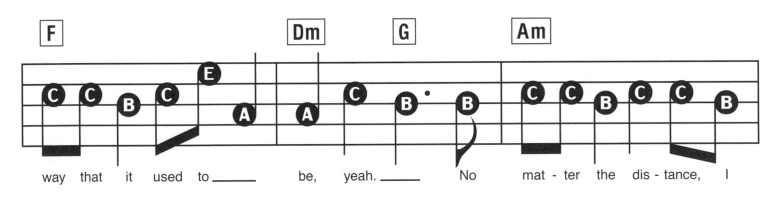

hear you say _____ I want it that _____ way. Am

CODA

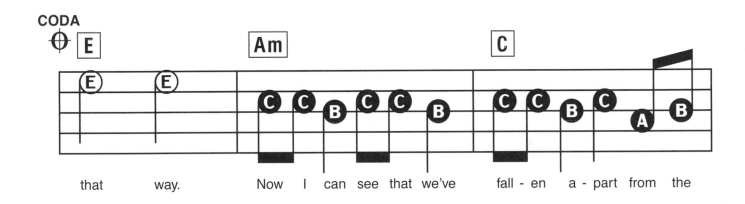

that way. Now I can see that we've fall - en a - part from the

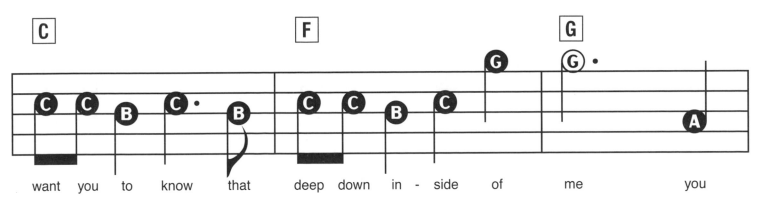

way that it used to _____ be, yeah. _____ No mat - ter the dis - tance, I

want you to know that deep down in - side of me you

76

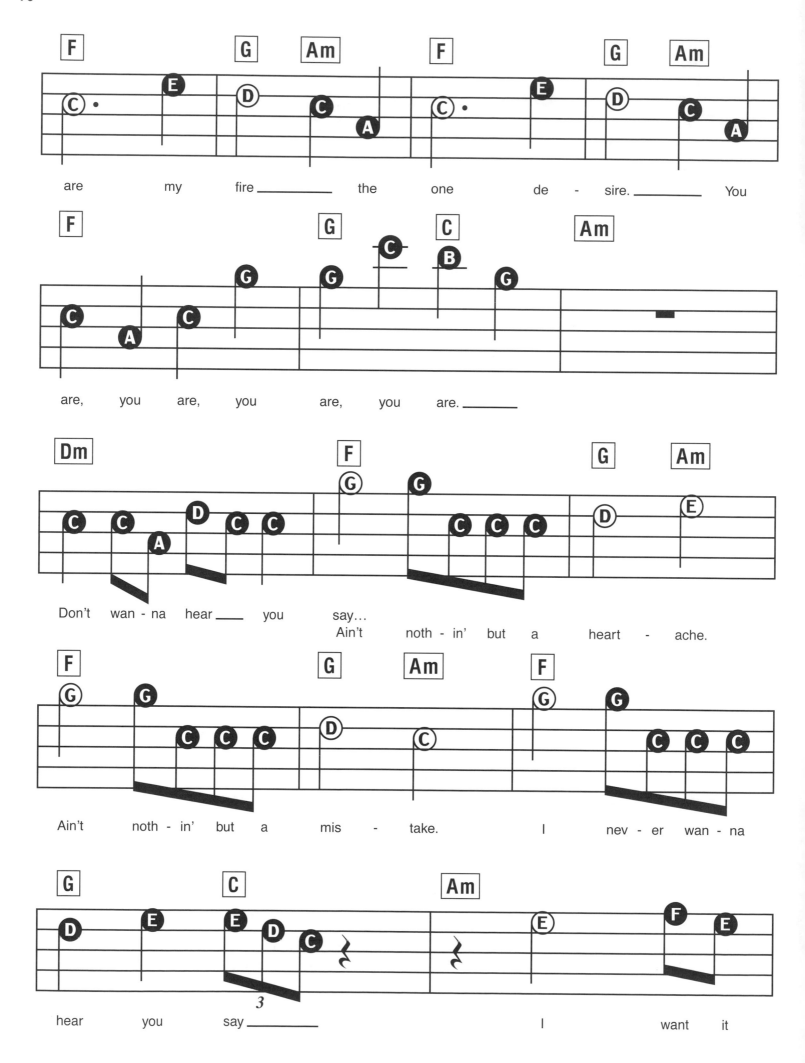

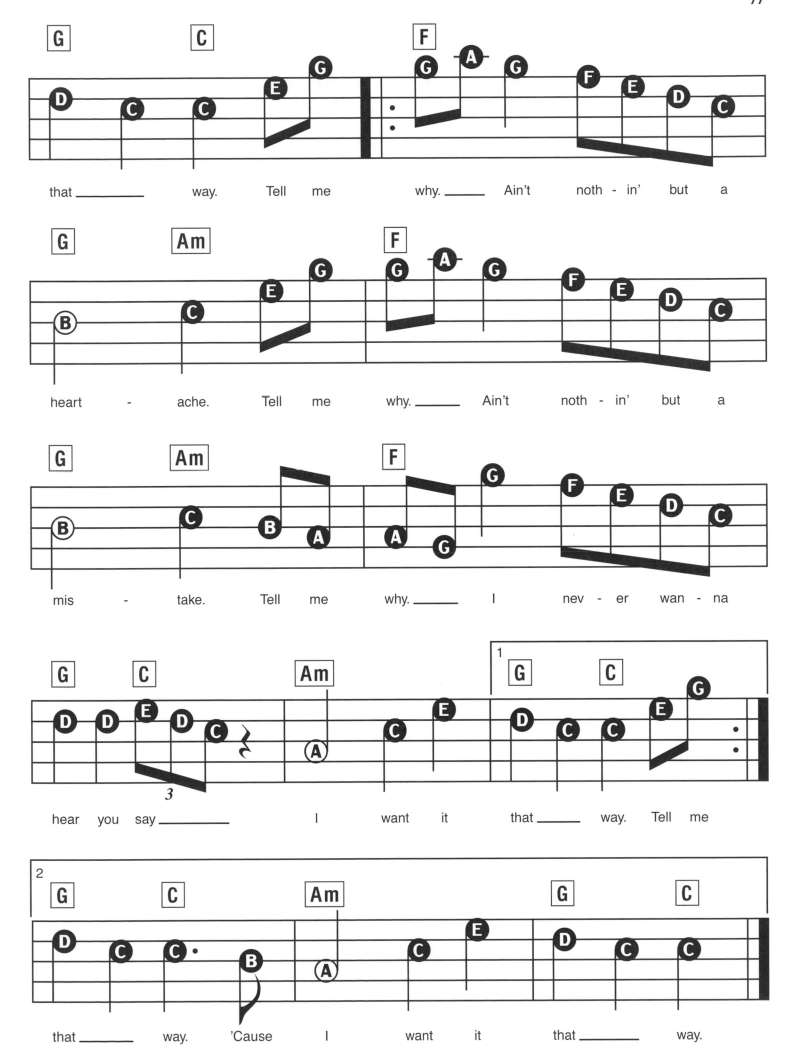

The Imperial March
(Darth Vader's Theme)
from THE EMPIRE STRIKES BACK

Registration 2
Rhythm: March

Music by
John Williams

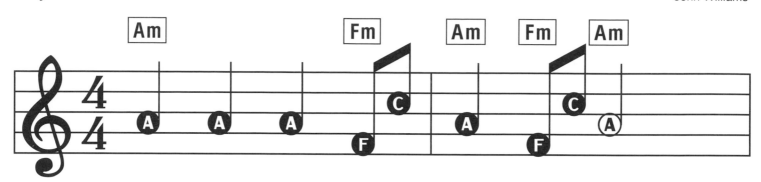

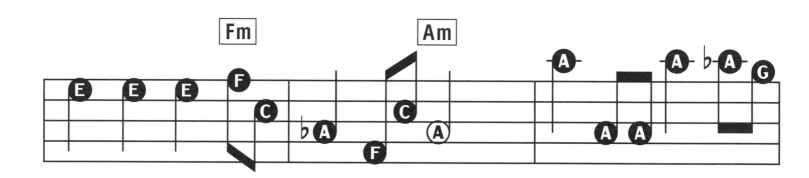

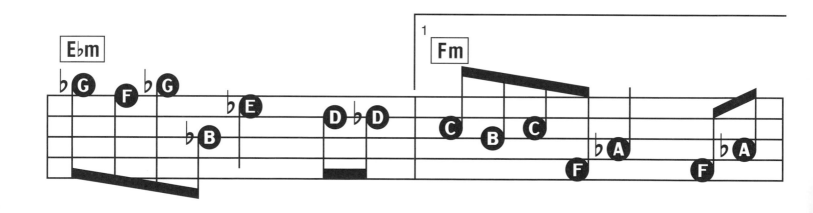

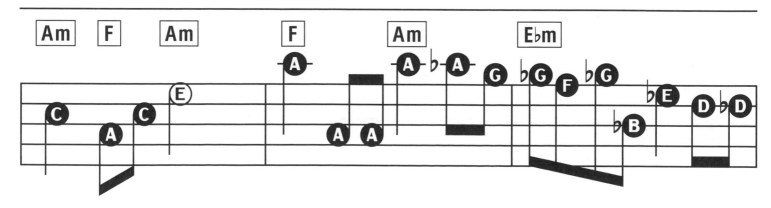

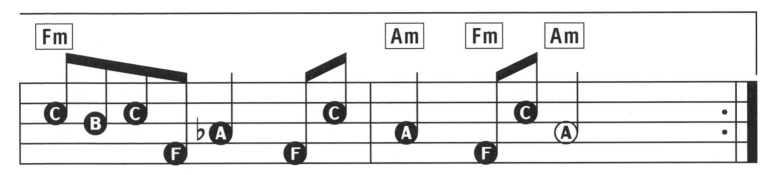

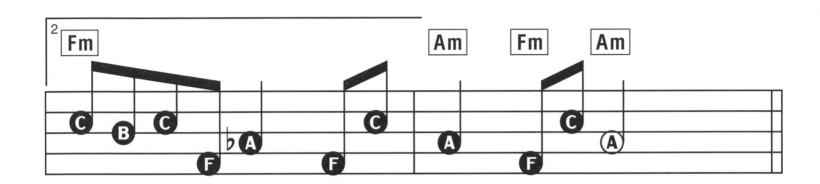

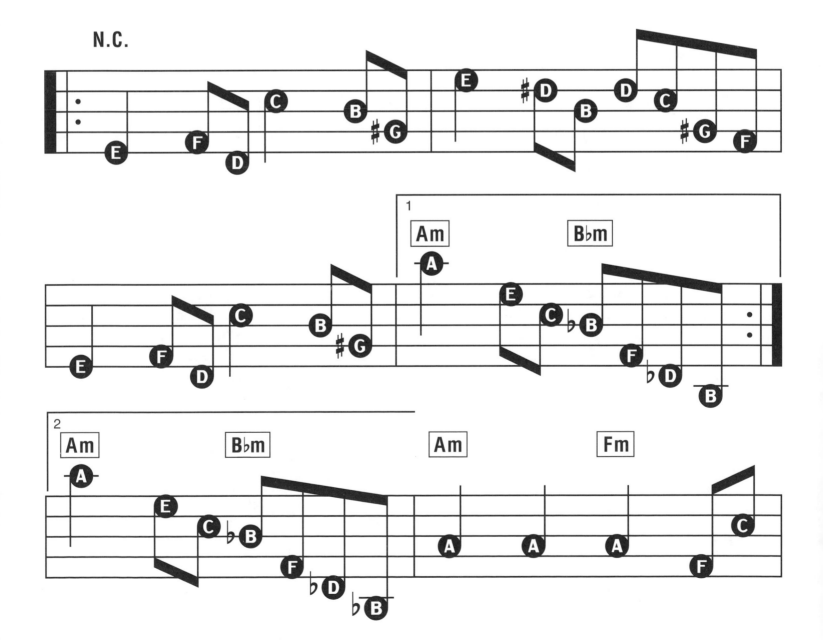

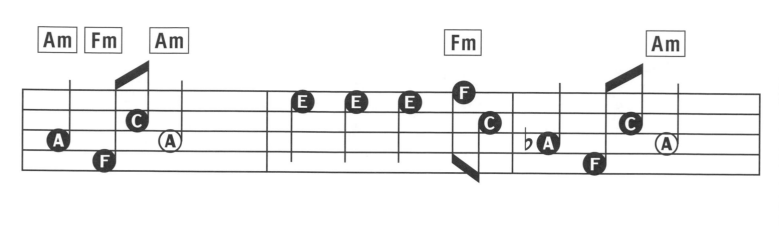

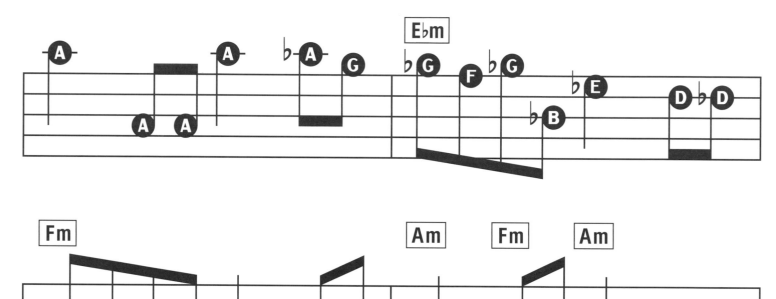

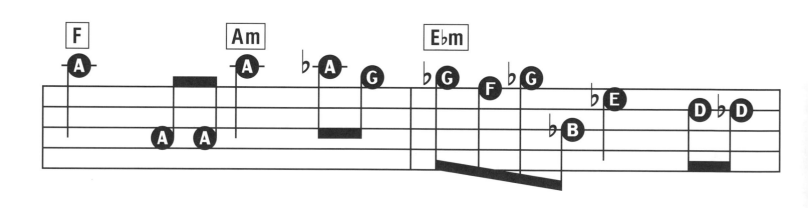

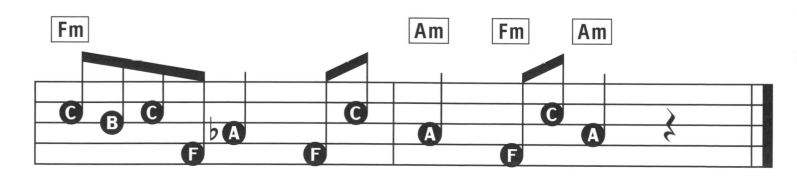

Imagine

Registration 8
Rhythm: Ballad

Words and Music by
John Lennon

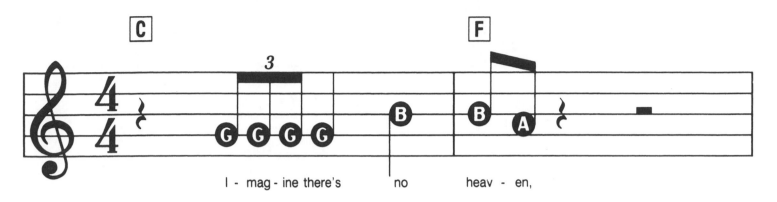

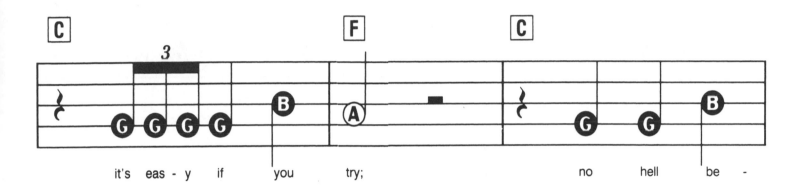

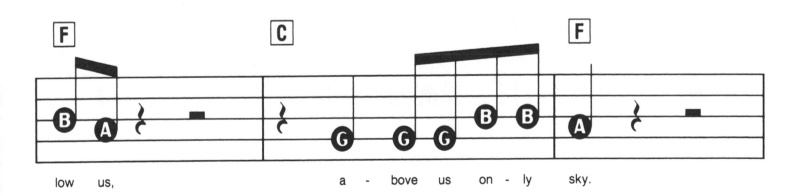

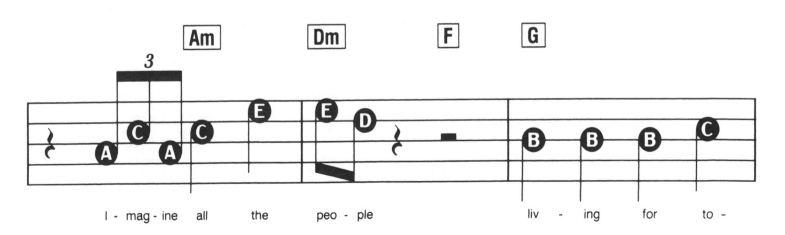

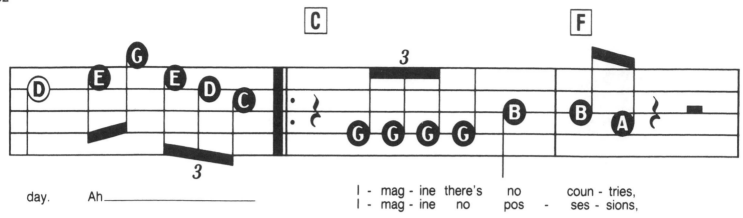

day. Ah_____

I - mag - ine there's no coun - tries,
I - mag - ine no pos - ses - sions,

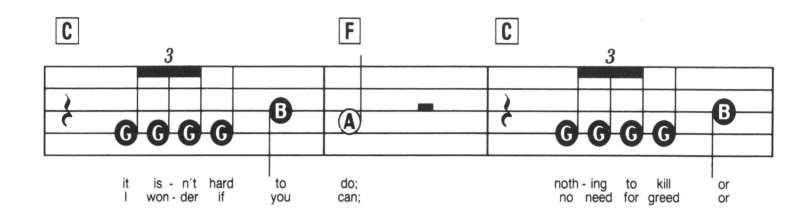

it is - n't hard to do;
I won - der if you can;

noth - ing to kill or
no need for greed or

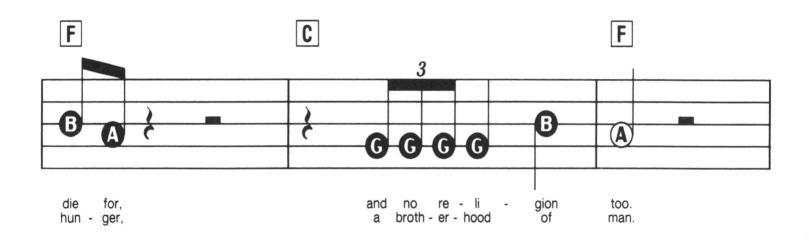

die for,
hun - ger,

and no re - li - gion too.
a broth - er - hood of man.

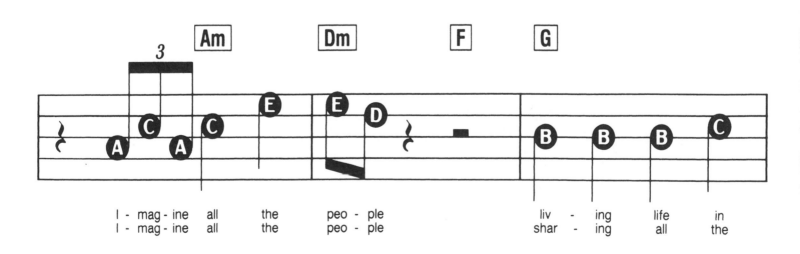

I - mag - ine all the peo - ple
I - mag - ine all the peo - ple

liv - ing life in
shar - ing all in the

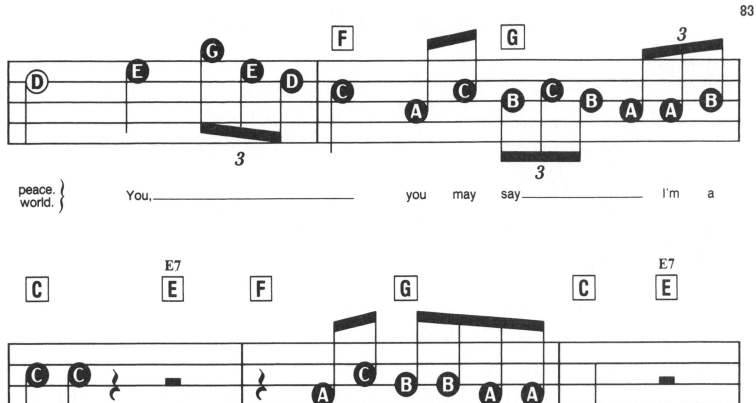

peace.
world.
} You,_____ you may say_____ I'm a

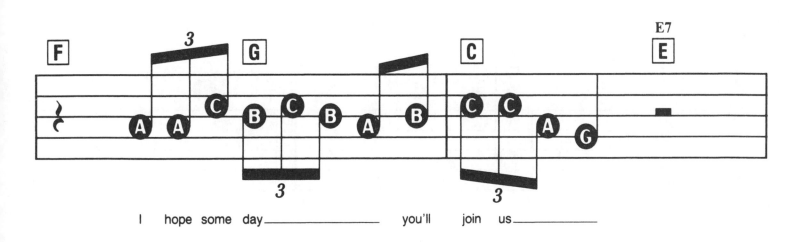

dream-er, but I'm not the on-ly one.

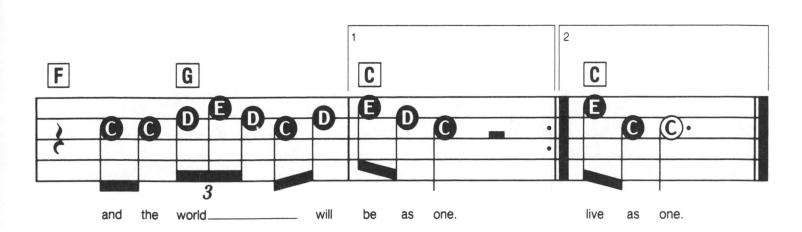

I hope some day_____ you'll join us_____

and the world_____ will be as one.

live as one.

Jeopardy Theme

Registration 7
Rhythm: Rock

Music by Merv Griffin

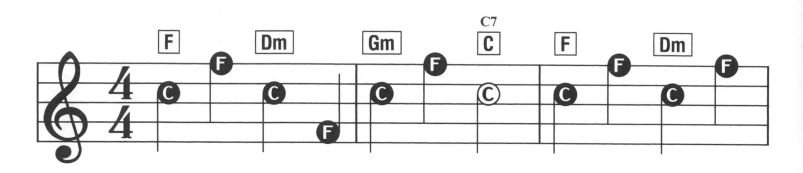

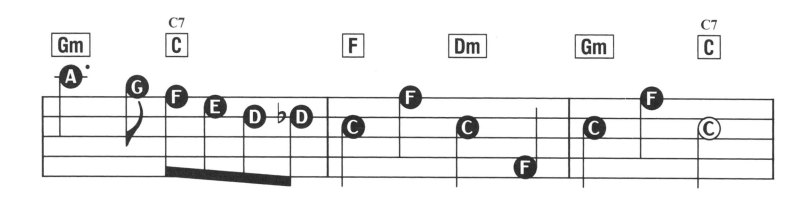

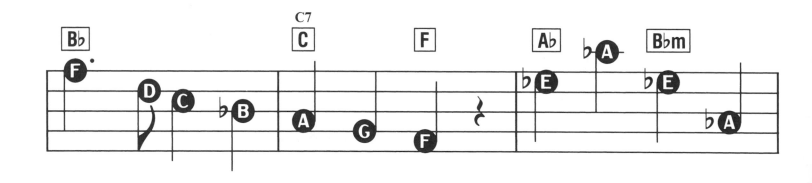

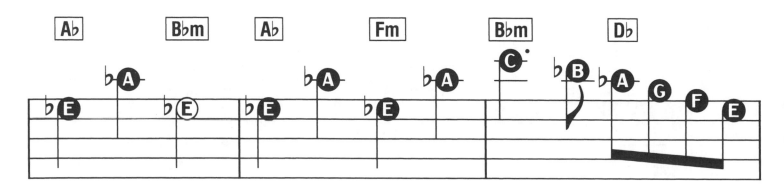

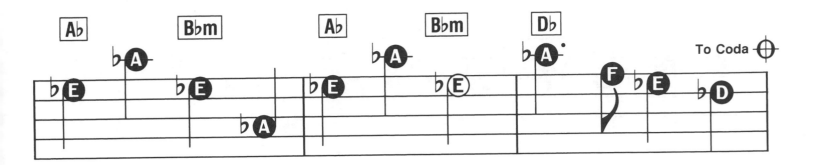

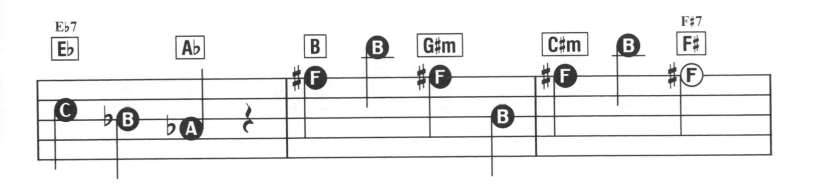

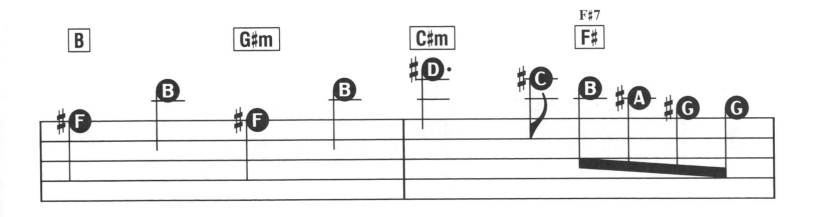

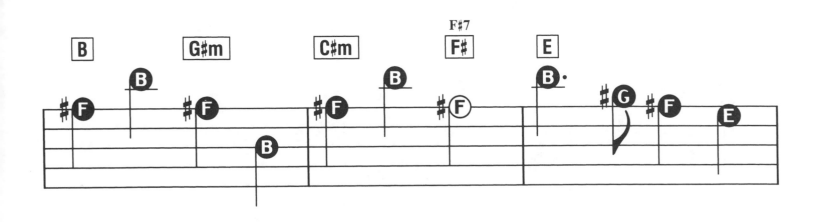

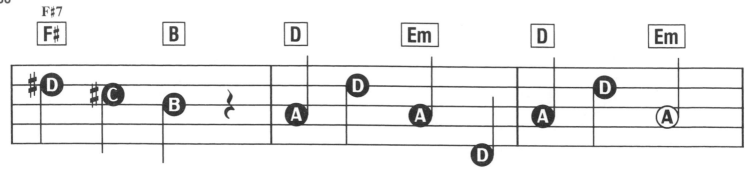

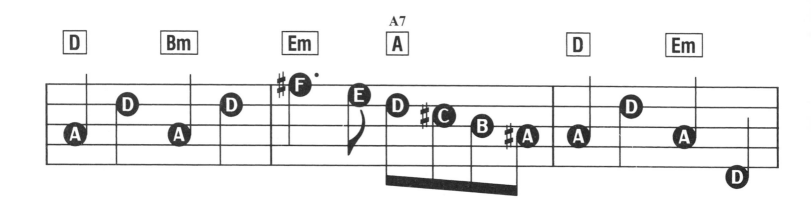

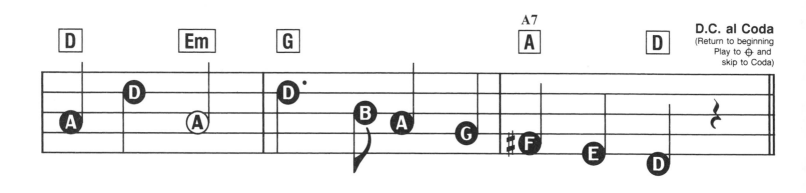

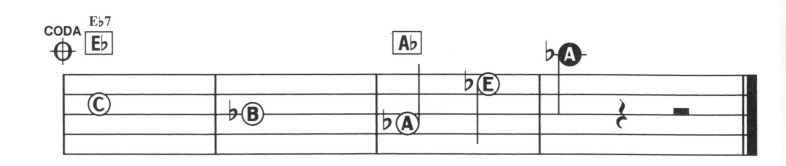

Theme from "Jurassic Park"
from the Universal Motion Picture JURASSIC PARK

Registration 8
Rhythm: Rock or 8-Beat

Composed by
John Williams

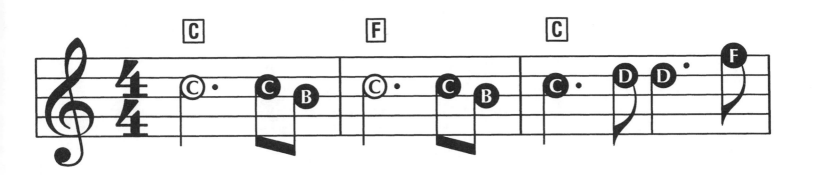

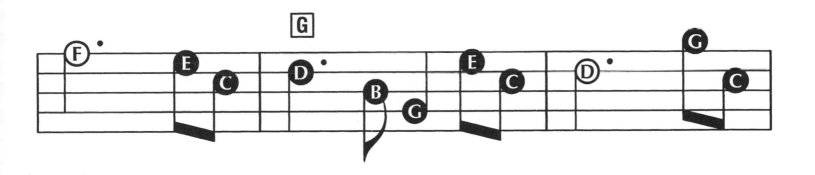

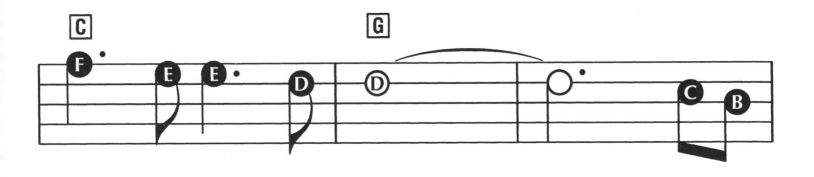

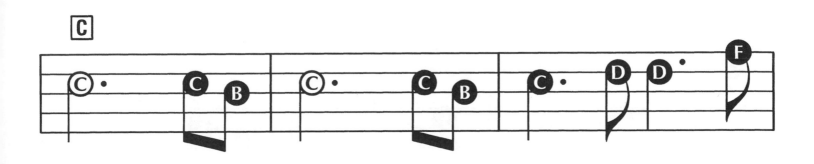

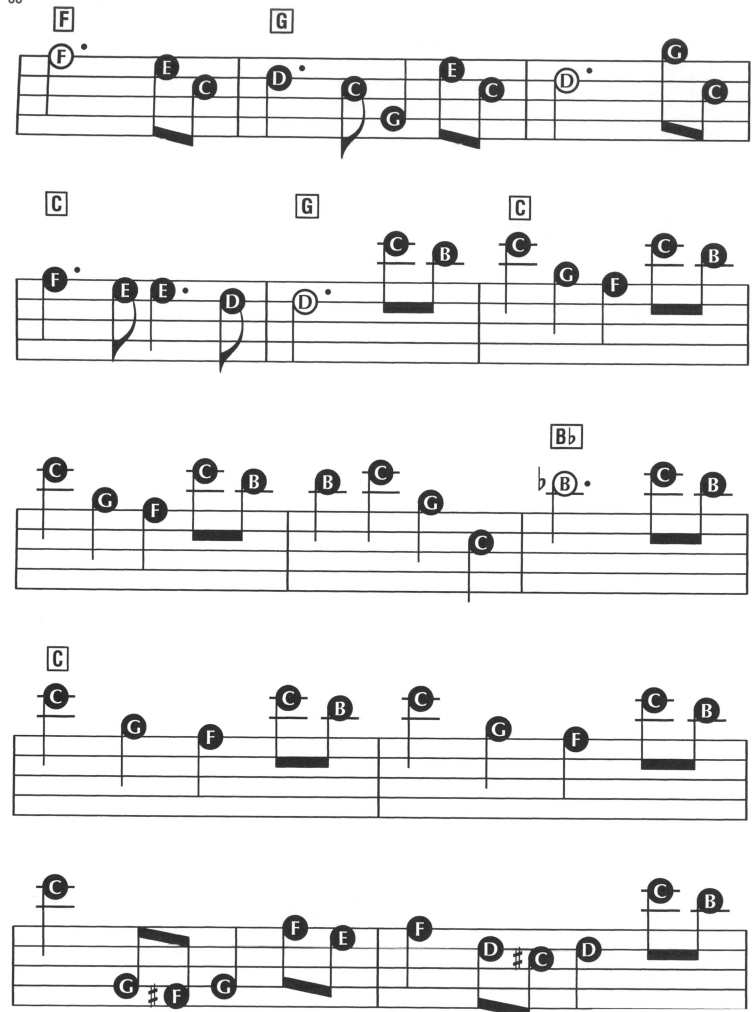

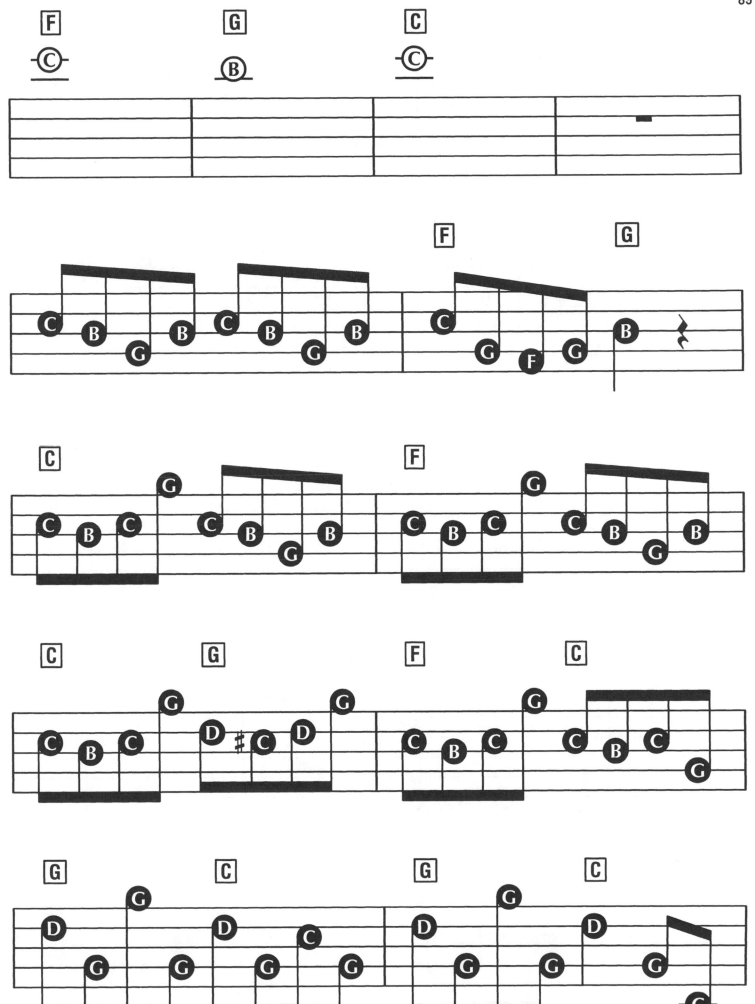

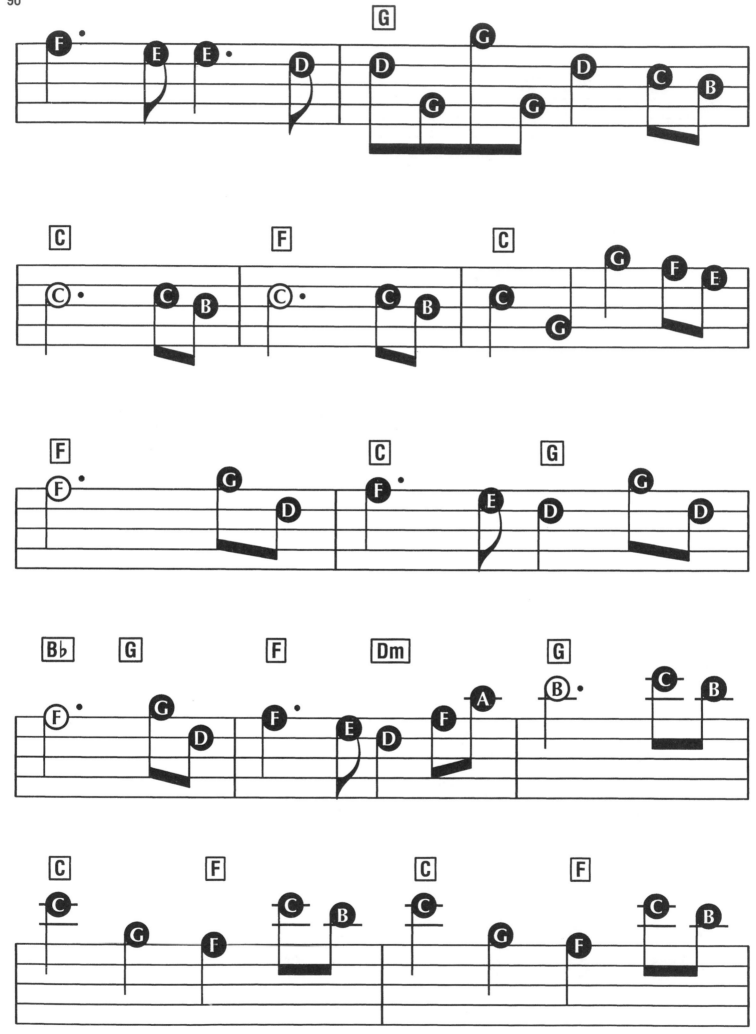

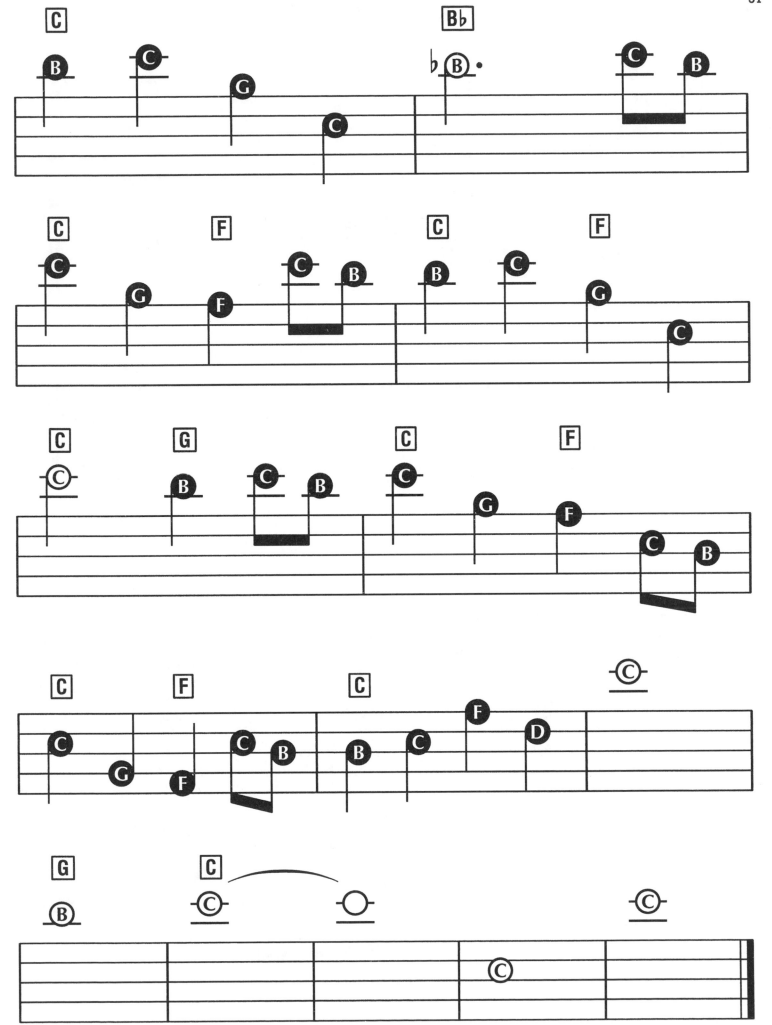

Lean on Me

Registration 8
Rhythm: Rock or 8-Beat

Words and Music by
Bill Withers

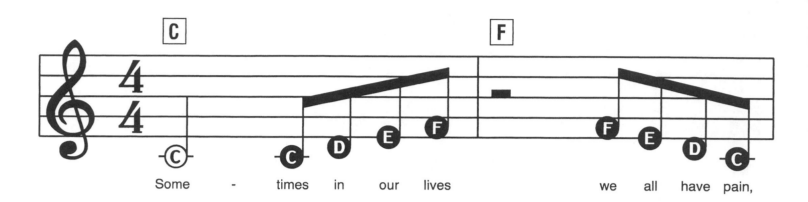

Some - times in our lives we all have pain,

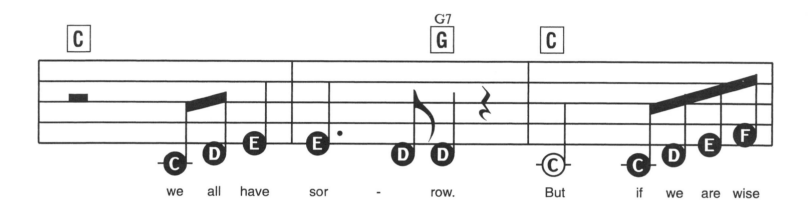

we all have sor - row. But if we are wise

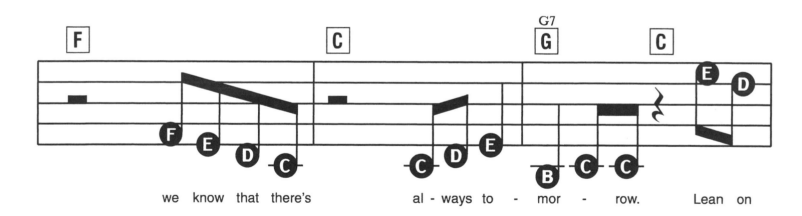

we know that there's al - ways to - mor - row. Lean on

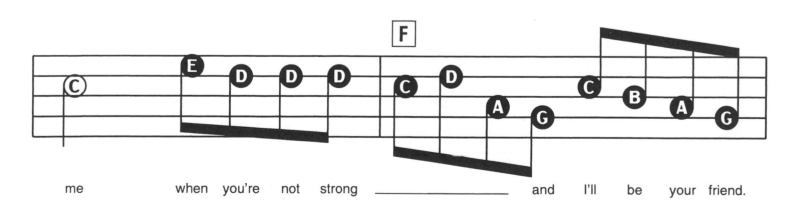

me when you're not strong _____ and I'll be your friend.

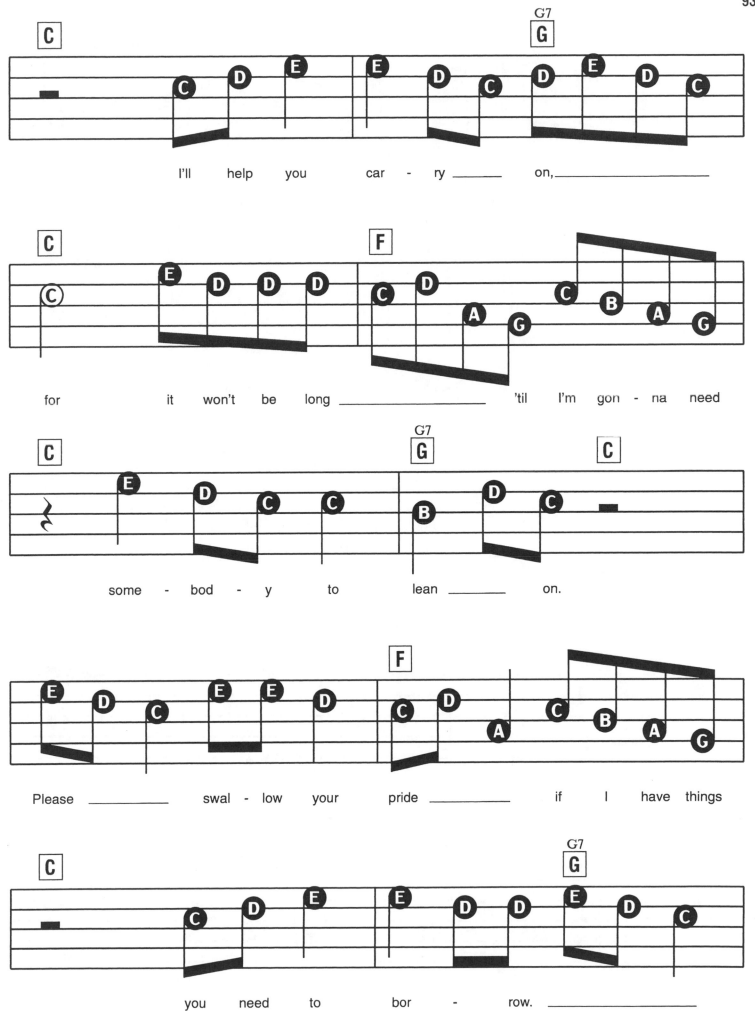

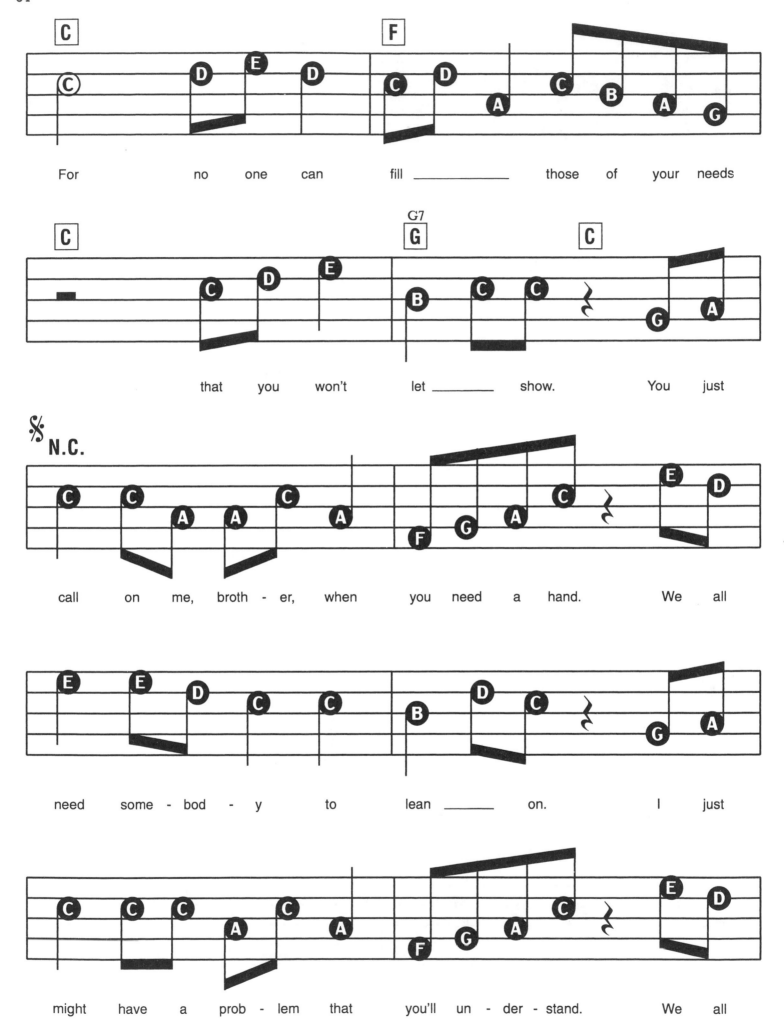

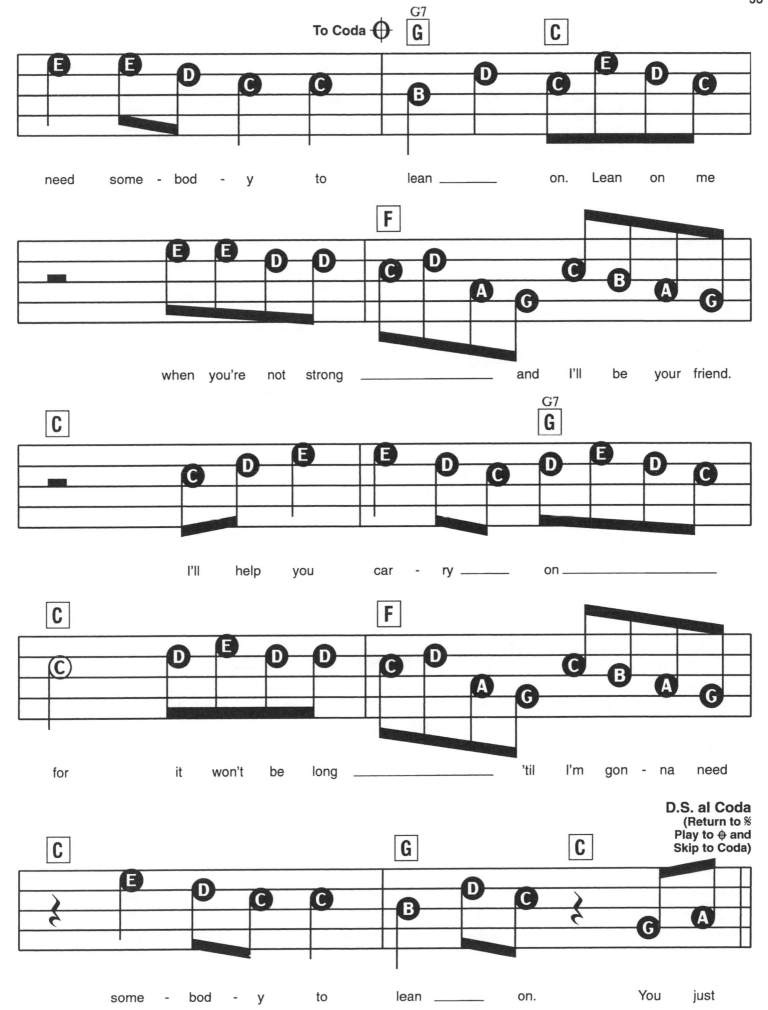

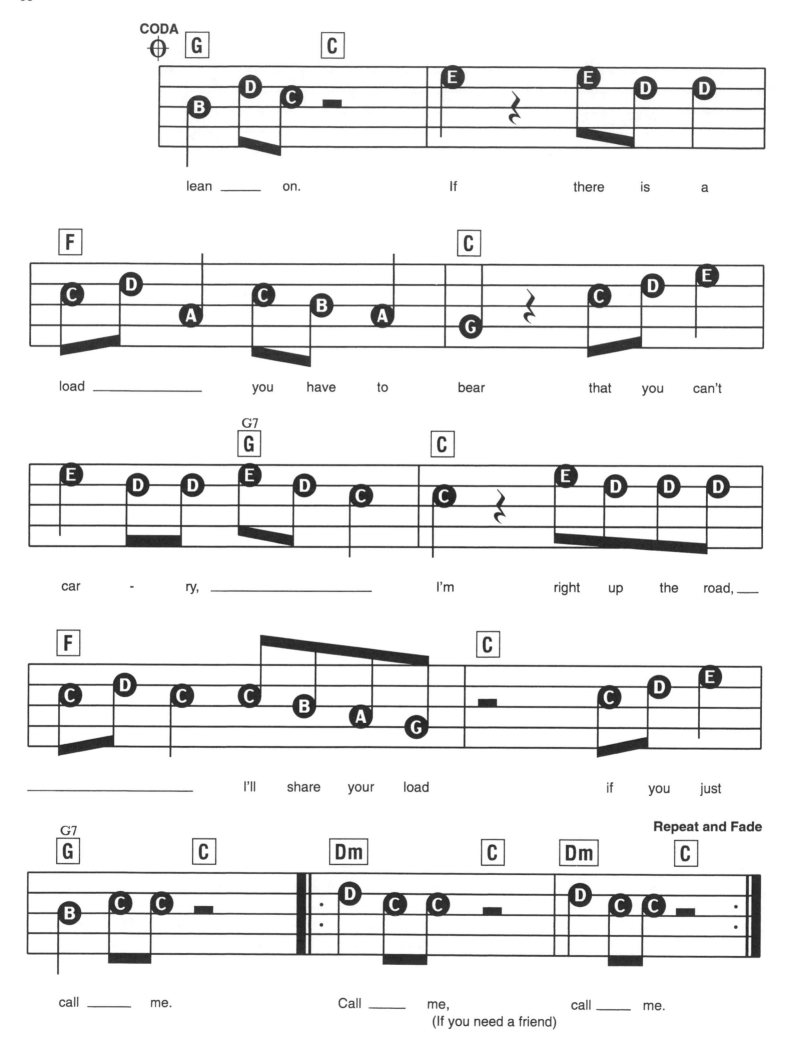

Let It Go
from FROZEN

Registration 8
Rhythm: Rock or Dance

Music and Lyrics by Kristen Anderson-Lopez
and Robert Lopez

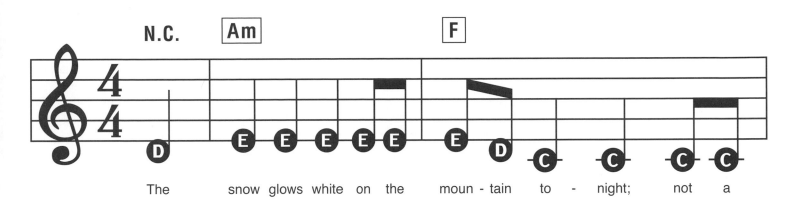

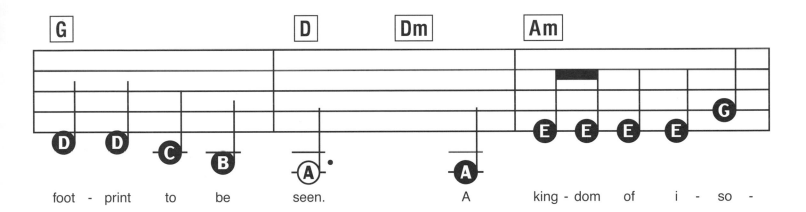

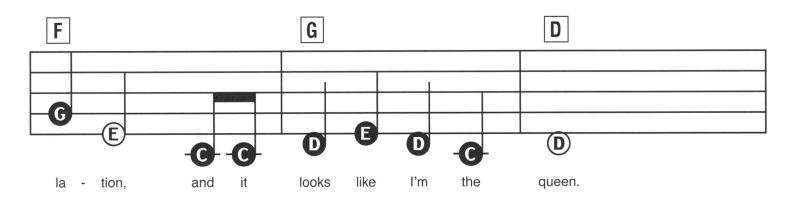

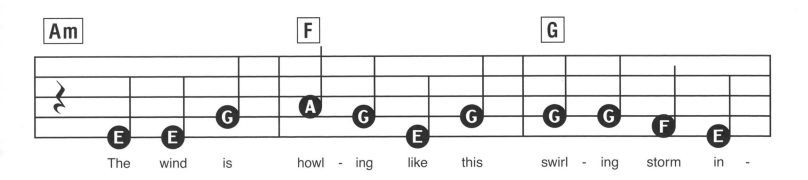

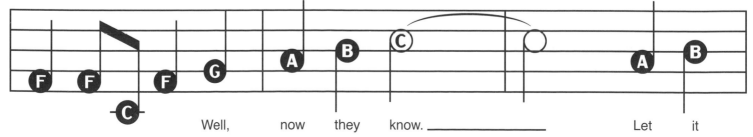

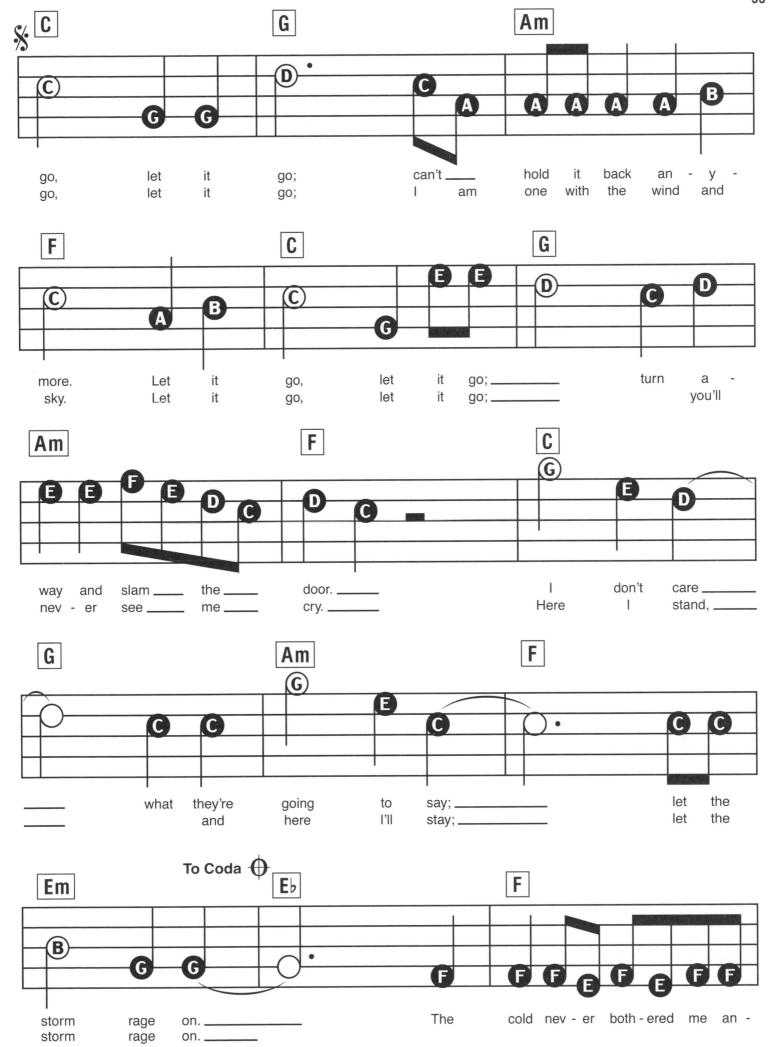

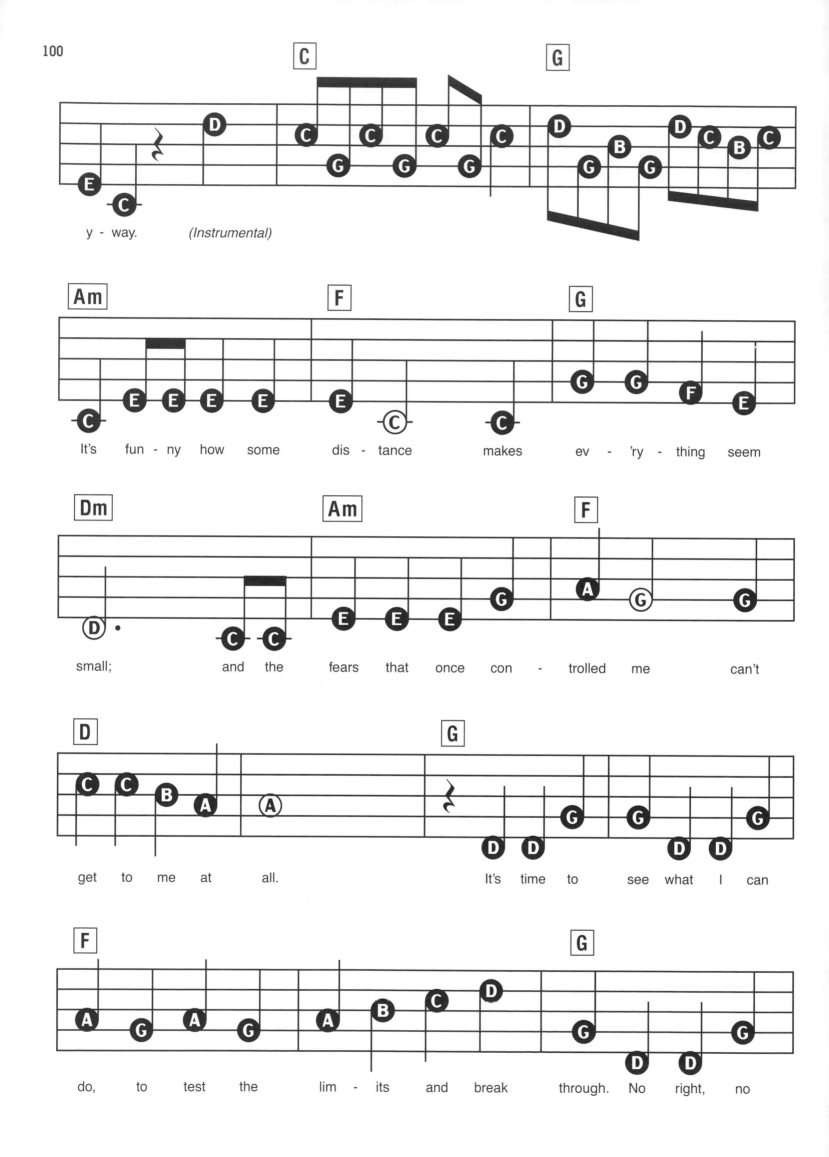

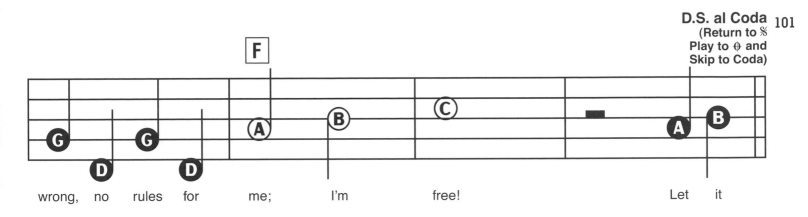

wrong, no rules for me; I'm free! Let it

CODA

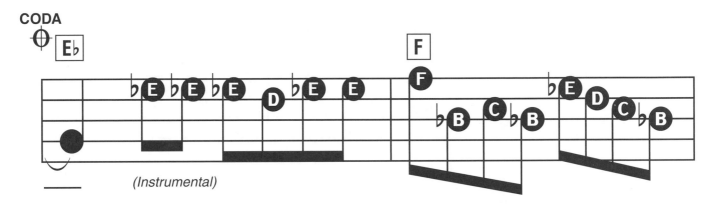

(Instrumental)

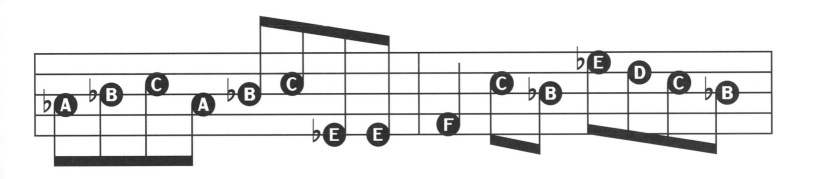

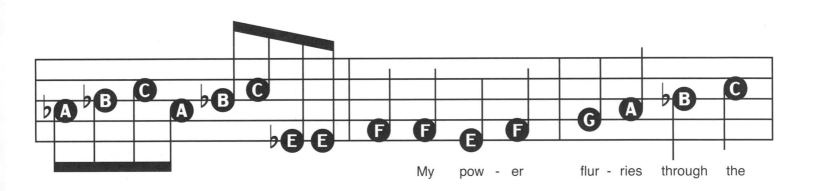

My pow - er flur - ries through the

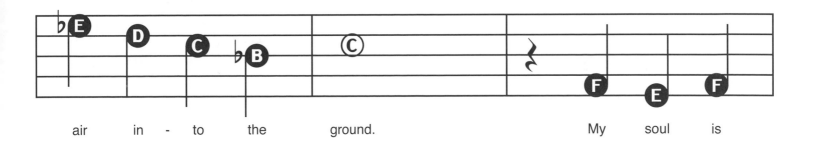

air in - to the ground. My soul is

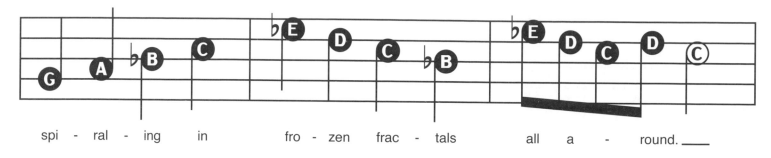

spi - ral - ing in fro - zen frac - tals all a - round. ___

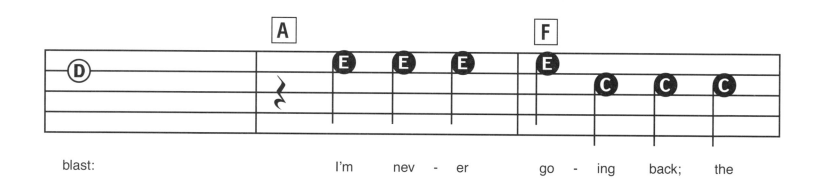

And one thought crys - tal - liz - es like an ic - y

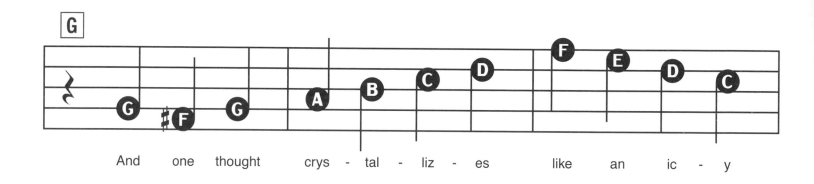

blast: I'm nev - er go - ing back; the

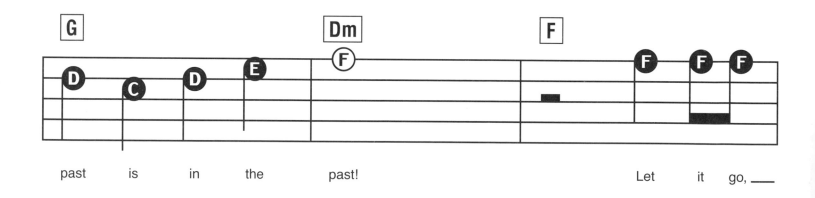

past is in the past! Let it go, ___

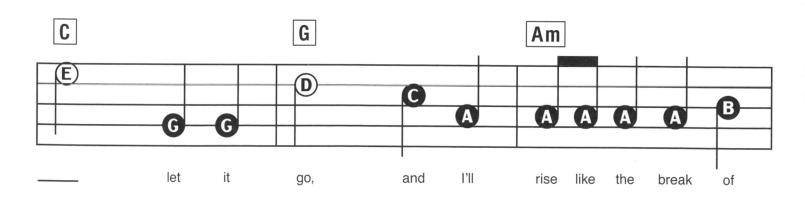

___ let it go, and I'll rise like the break of

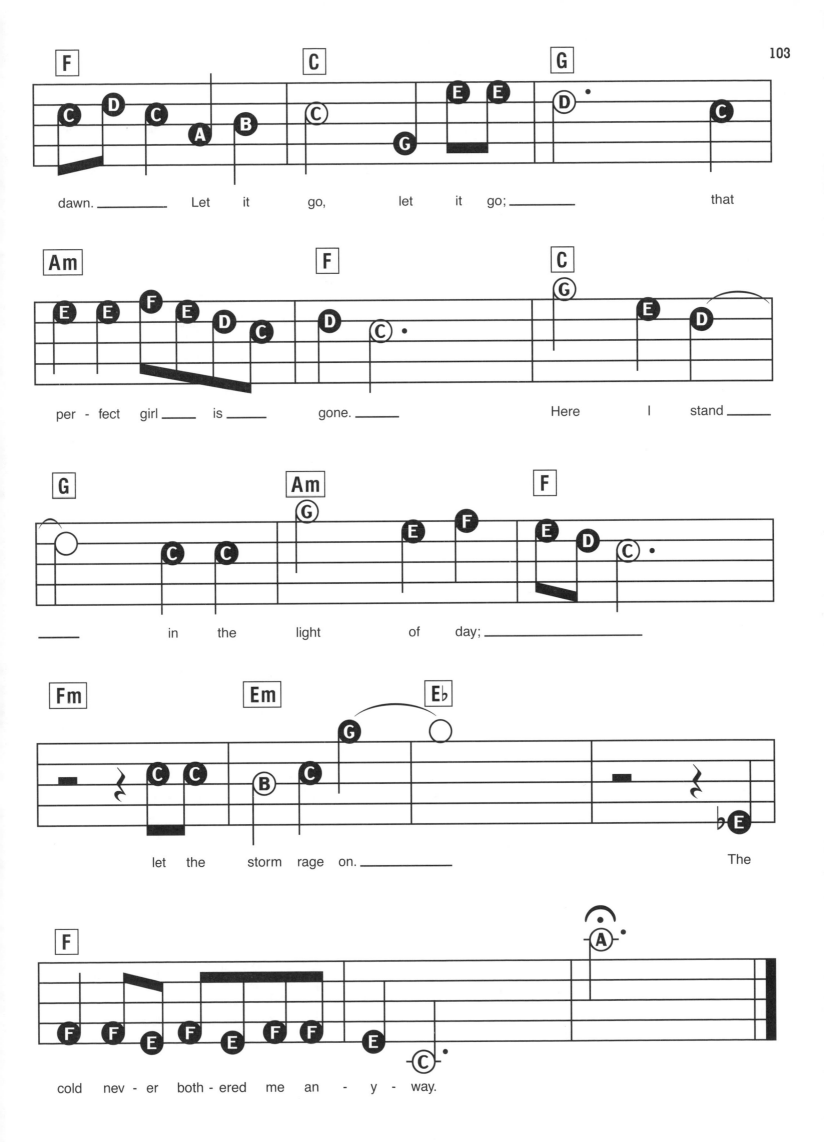

Let It Be

Registration 3
Rhythm: Rock or Pops

Words and Music by John Lennon
and Paul McCartney

When I find my-self in times of trou-ble, Moth-er Mar-y comes to me, speak-ing words of wis-dom, let it be. _____ And in my hour of dark-ness she is stand-ing right in front of me, speak-ing words of wis-dom, let it be. _____ Let it

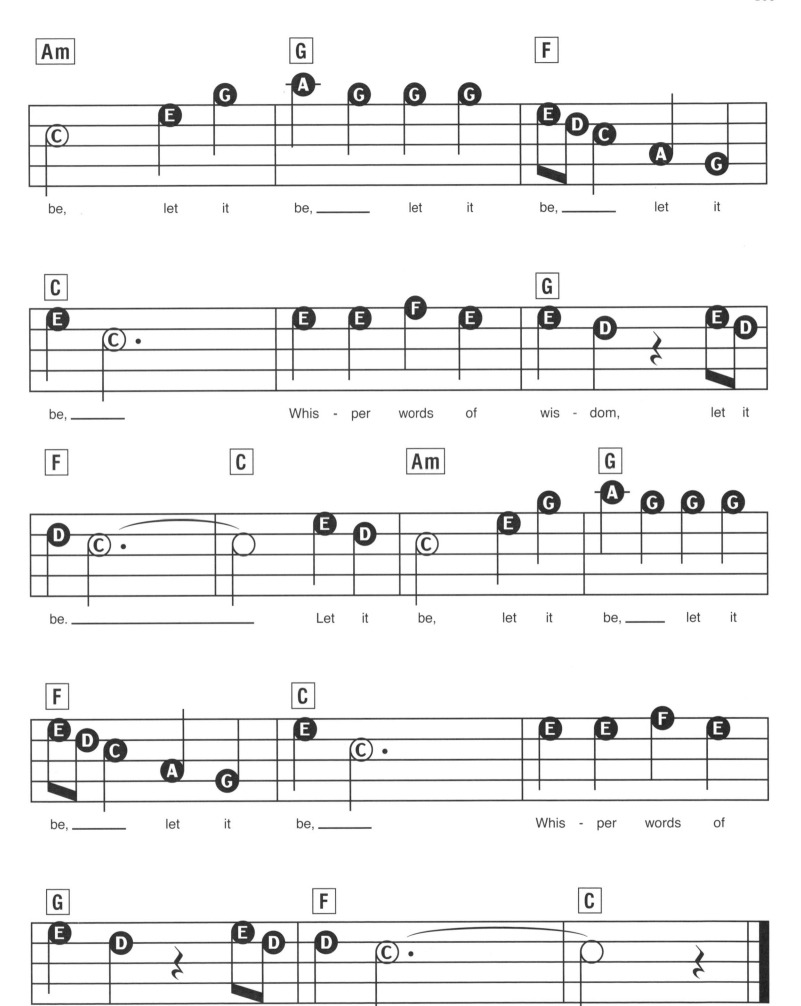

Linus and Lucy
from A CHARLIE BROWN CHRISTMAS

Registration 8
Rhythm: Fox Trot or Swing

By Vince Guaraldi

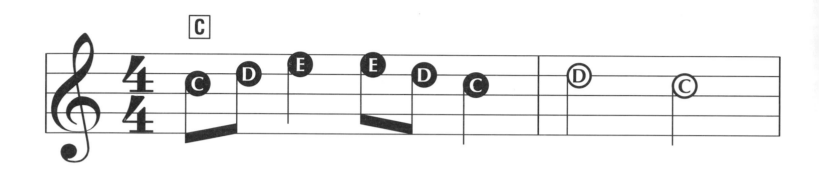

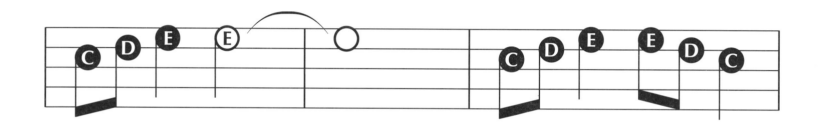

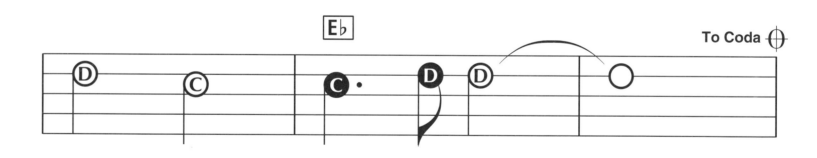

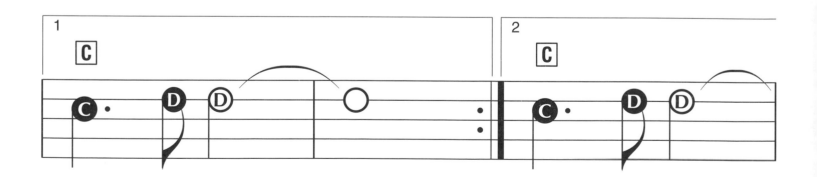

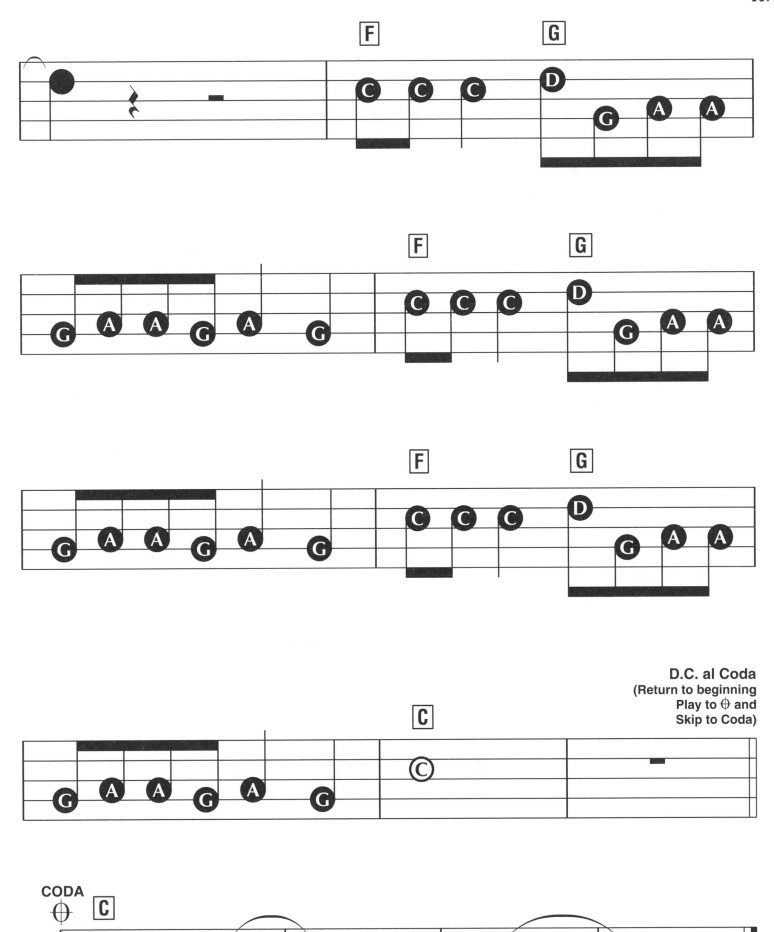

Minuet in G

Registration 8
Rhythm: Waltz or None

By Johann Sebastian Bach

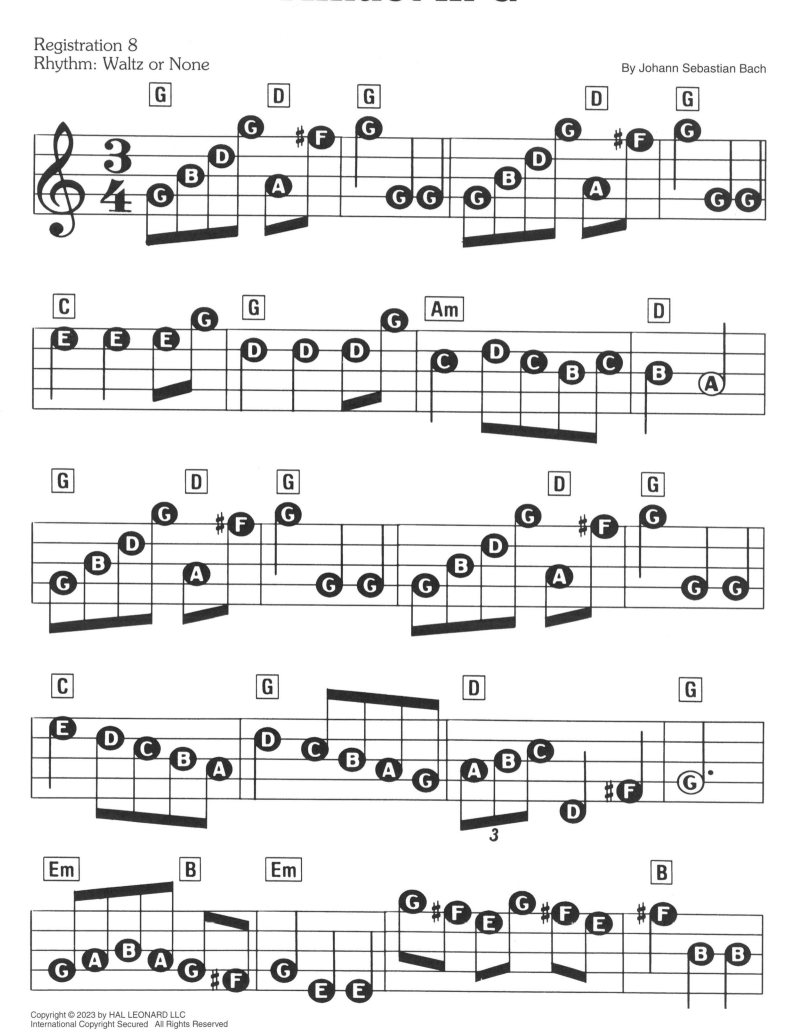

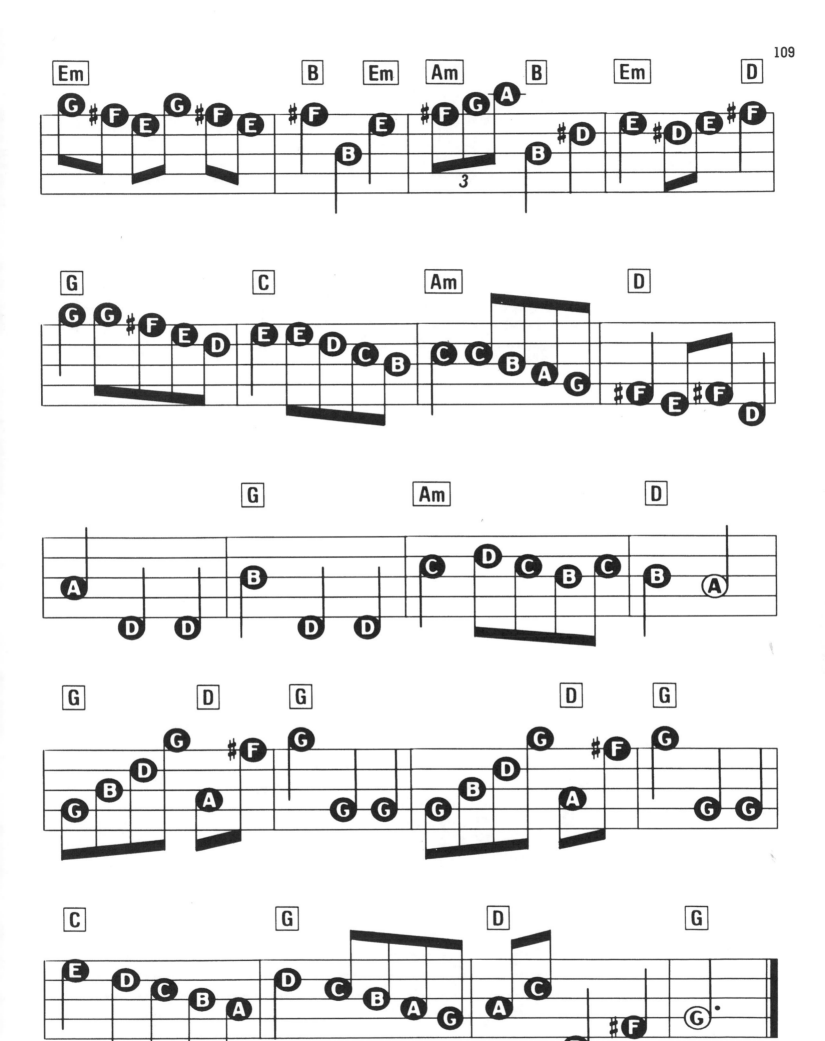

Mission: Impossible Theme

from the Paramount Television Series MISSION: IMPOSSIBLE

Registration 2
Rhythm: Jazz Waltz or Waltz

By Lalo Schifrin

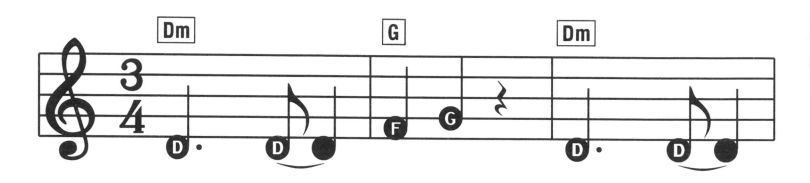

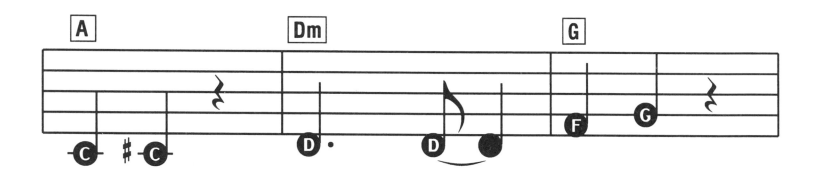

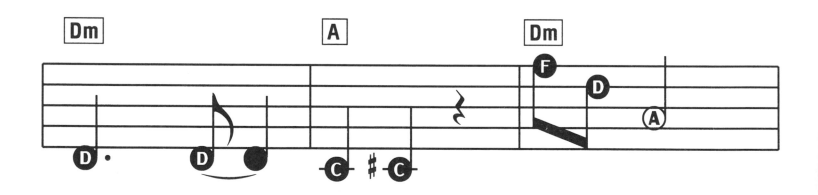

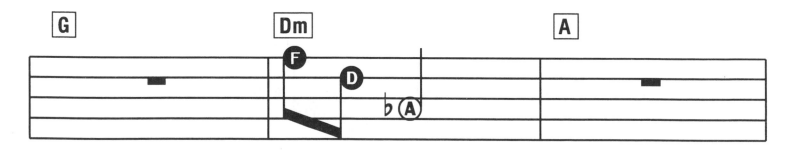

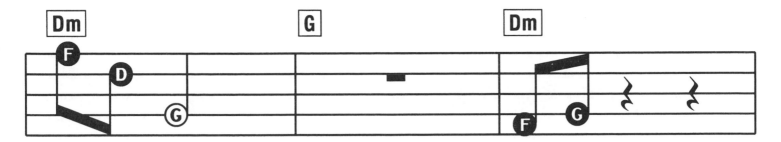

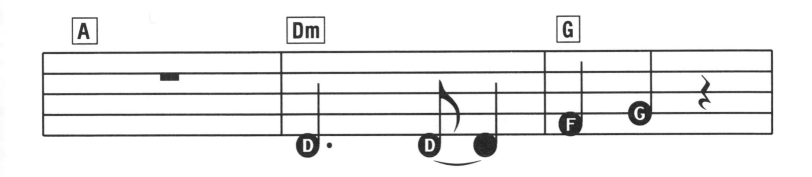

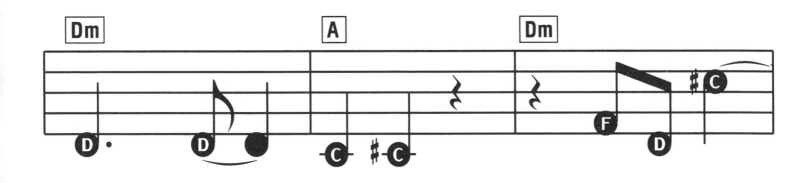

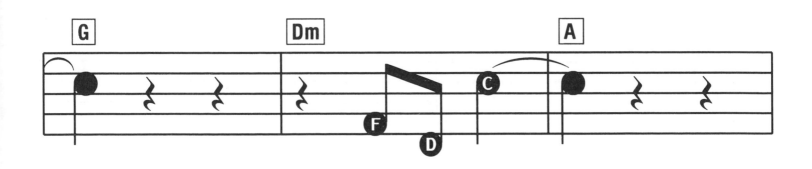

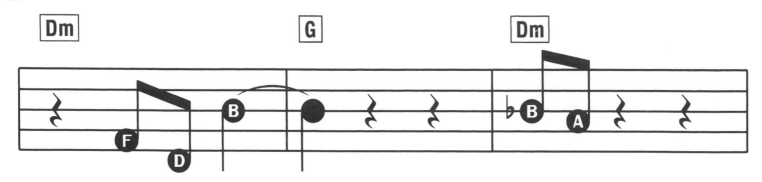

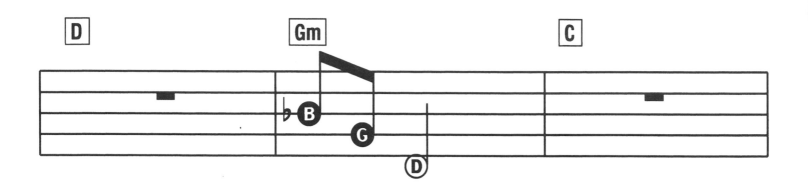

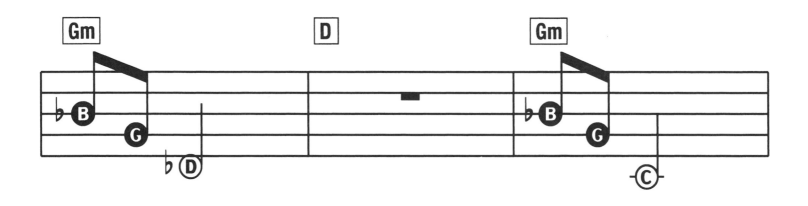

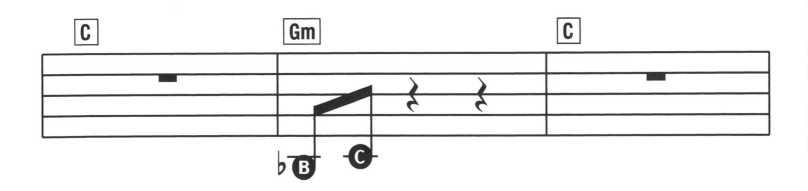

113

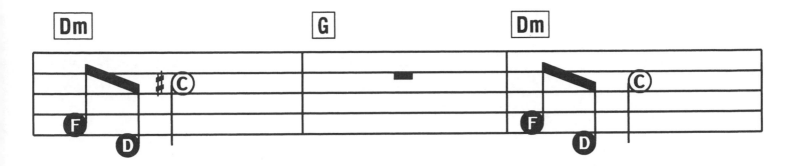

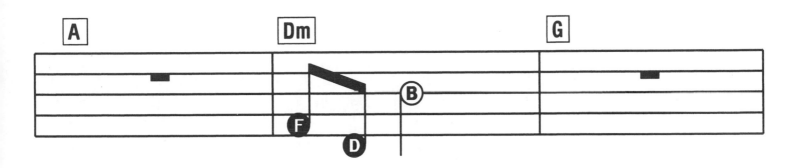

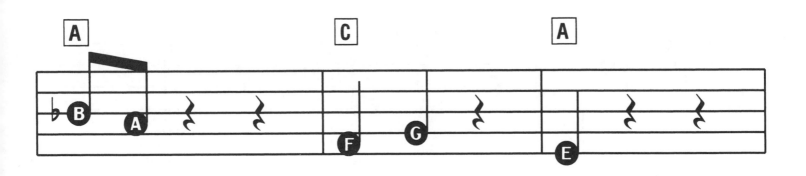

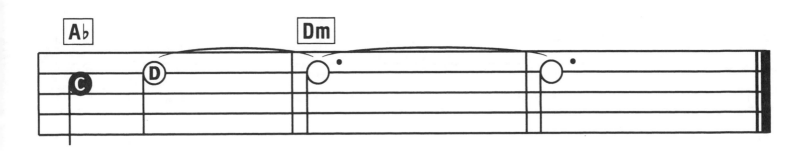

My Favorite Things
from THE SOUND OF MUSIC

Registration 1
Rhythm: Waltz

Lyrics by Oscar Hammerstein II
Music by Richard Rodgers

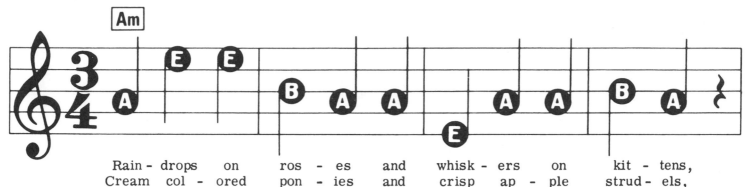

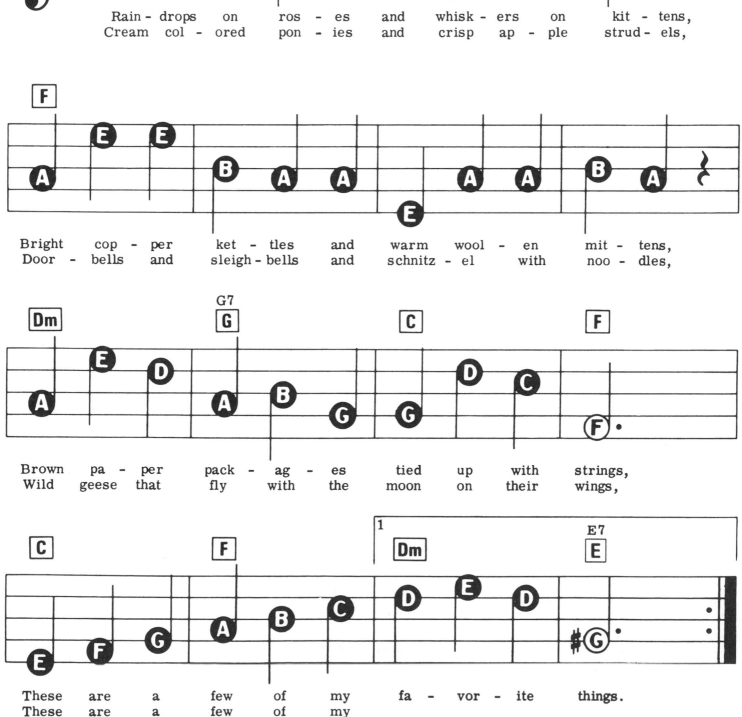

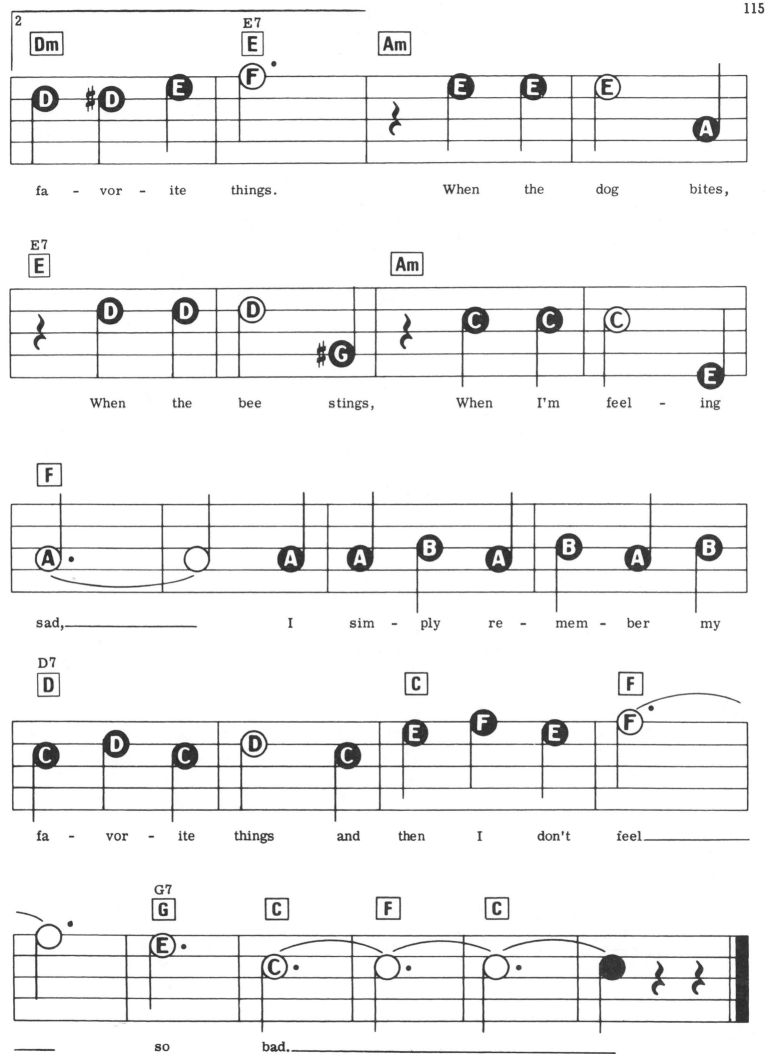

Over the Rainbow
from THE WIZARD OF OZ

Registration 5
Rhythm: Ballad

Music by Harold Arlen
Lyric by E.Y. "Yip" Harburg

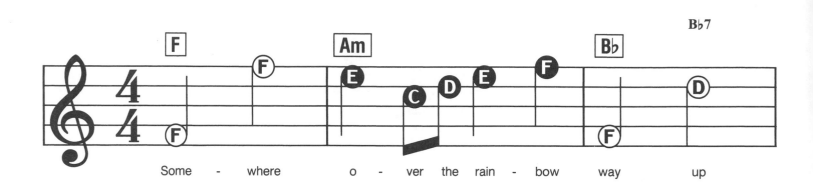

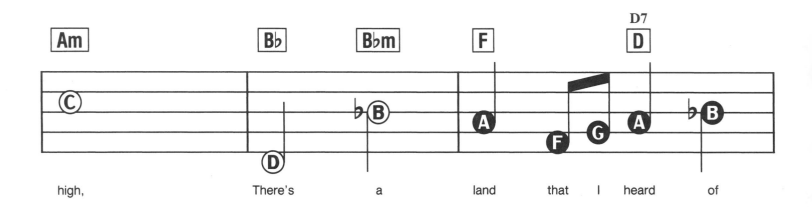

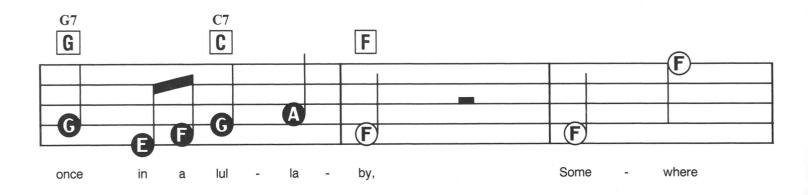

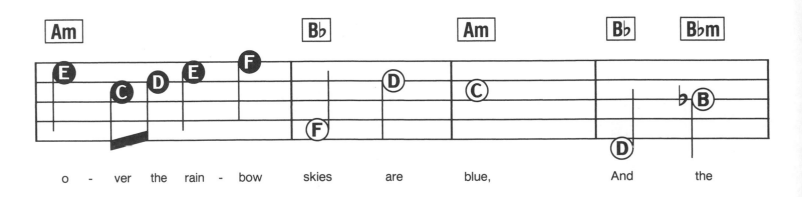

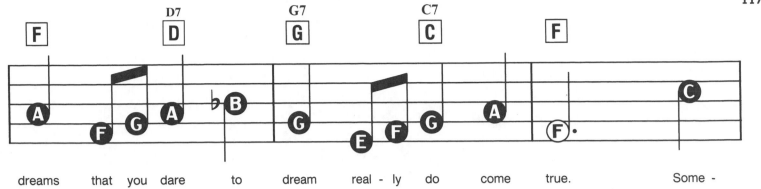

dreams   that   you   dare   to   dream   real - ly   do   come   true.   Some -

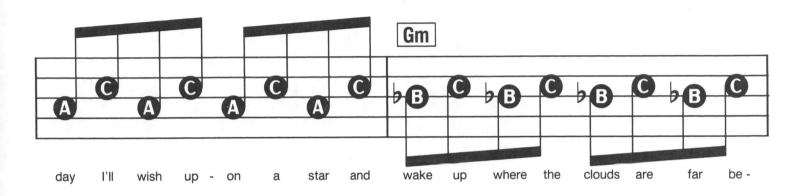

day   I'll   wish   up - on   a   star   and   wake   up   where   the   clouds   are   far   be -

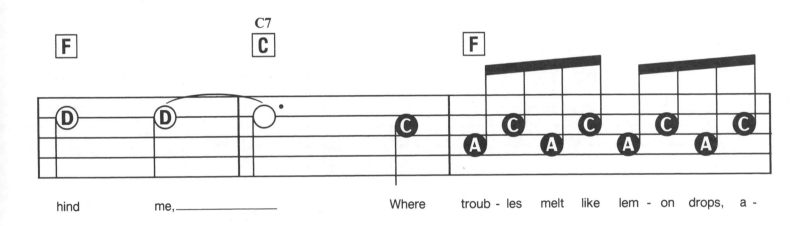

hind   me,_____   Where   troub - les   melt   like   lem - on   drops,   a -

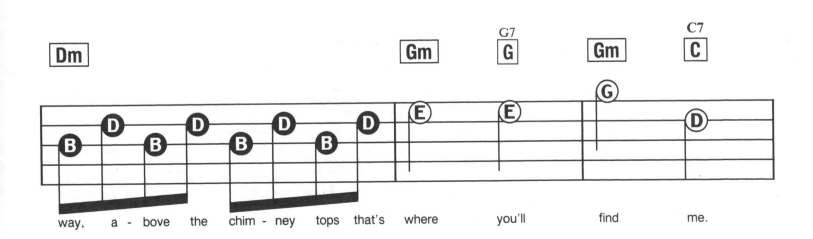

way,   a - bove   the   chim - ney   tops   that's   where   you'll   find   me.

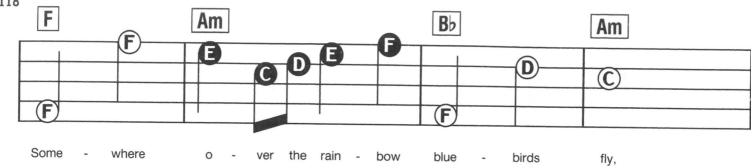

Some - where o - ver the rain - bow blue - birds fly,

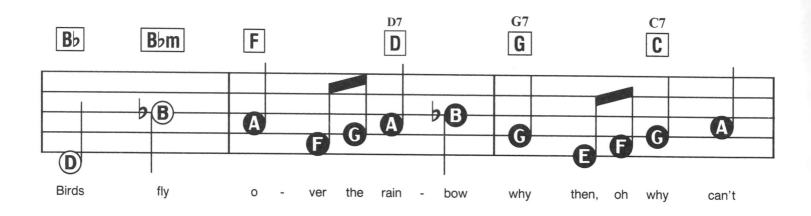

Birds fly o - ver the rain - bow why then, oh why can't

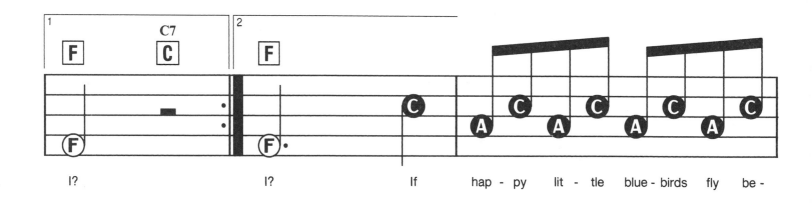

I? I? If hap - py lit - tle blue - birds fly be -

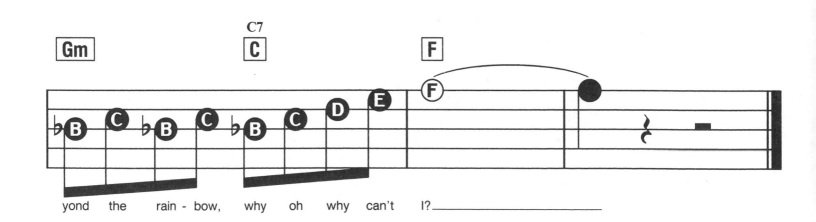

yond the rain - bow, why oh why can't I?_____

A Sky Full of Stars

Registration 8
Rhythm: Dance or Rock

Words and Music by Guy Berryman,
Jon Buckland, Will Champion,
Chris Martin and Tim Bergling

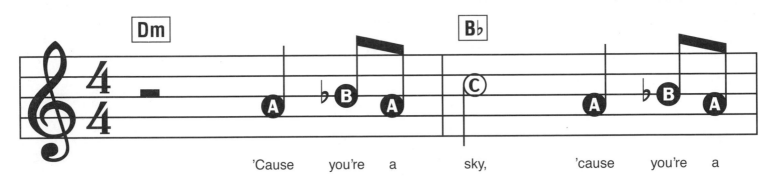

'Cause you're a sky, 'cause you're a

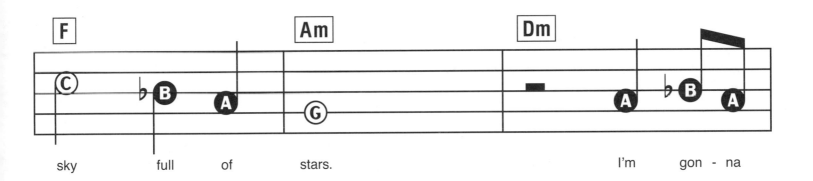

sky full of stars. I'm gon-na

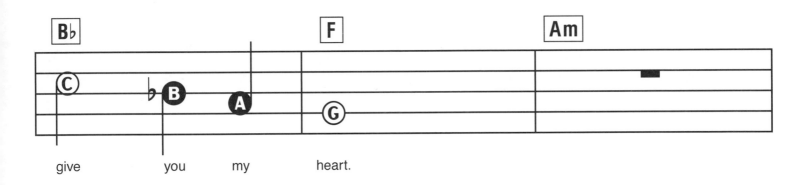

give you my heart.

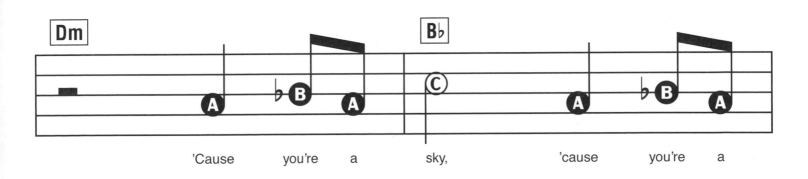

'Cause you're a sky, 'cause you're a

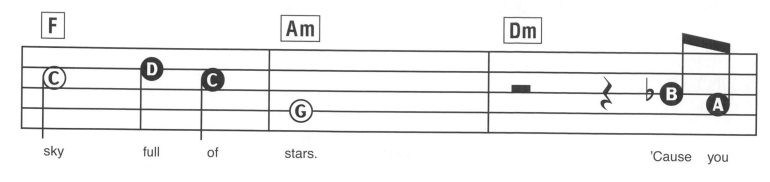

sky   full   of   stars.   'Cause you

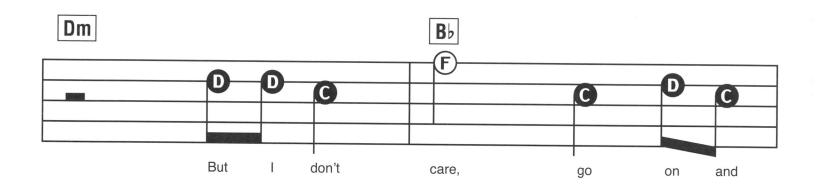

light   up   the   path. _____

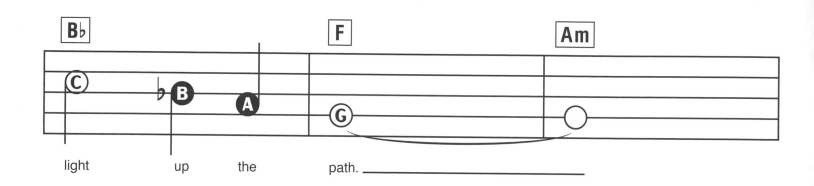

But   I   don't   care,   go   on   and

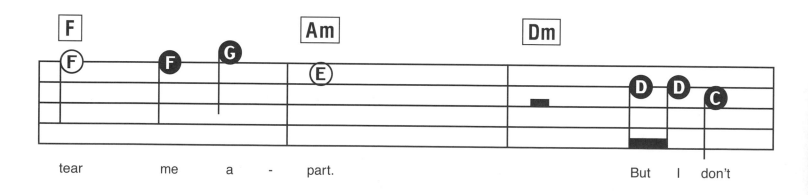

tear   me   a -   part.   But   I   don't

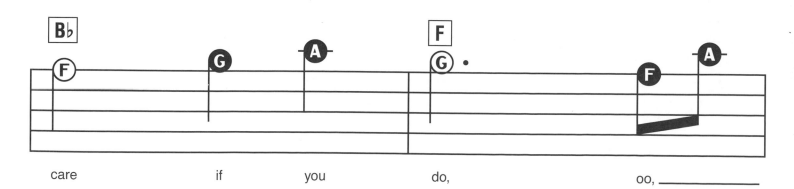

care   if   you   do,   oo, _____

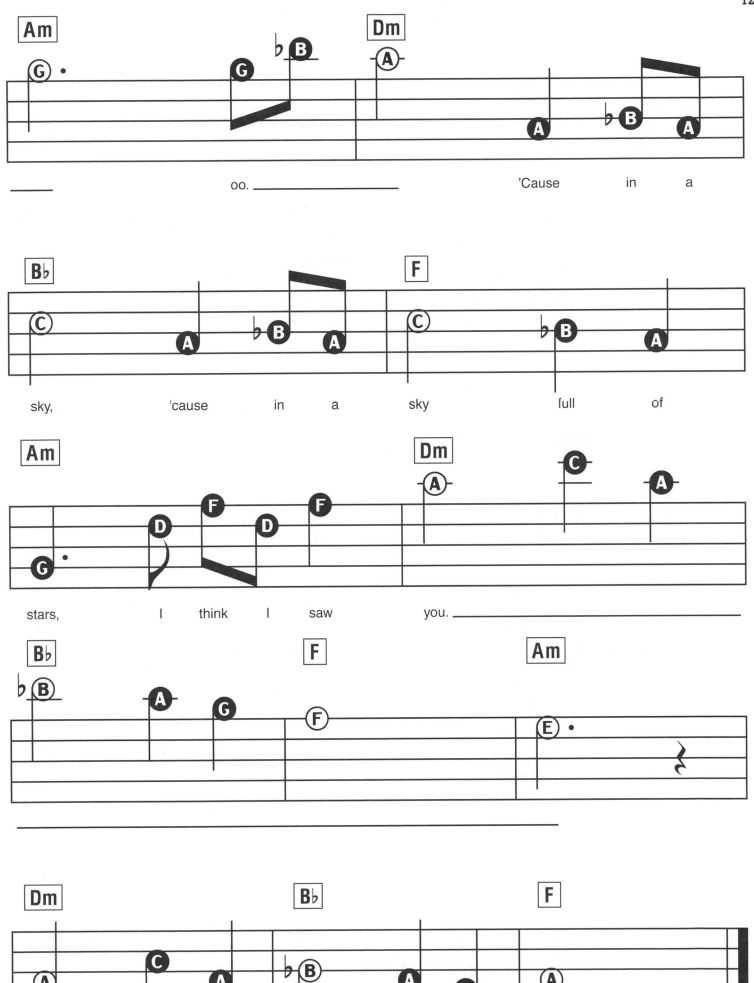

The Pink Panther
from THE PINK PANTHER

Registration 1
Rhythm: Swing

By Henry Mancini

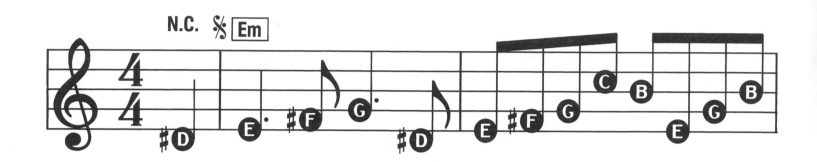

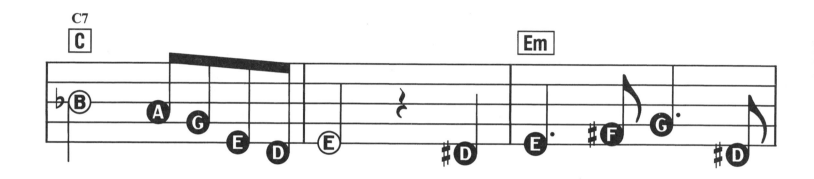

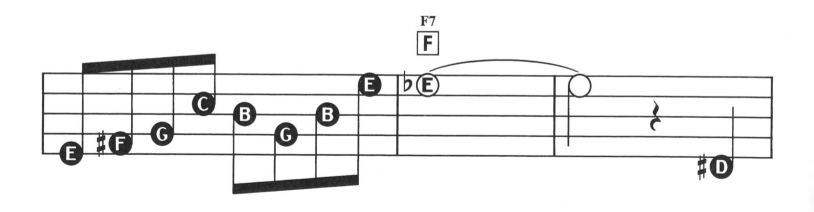

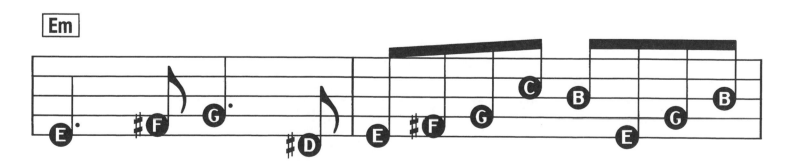

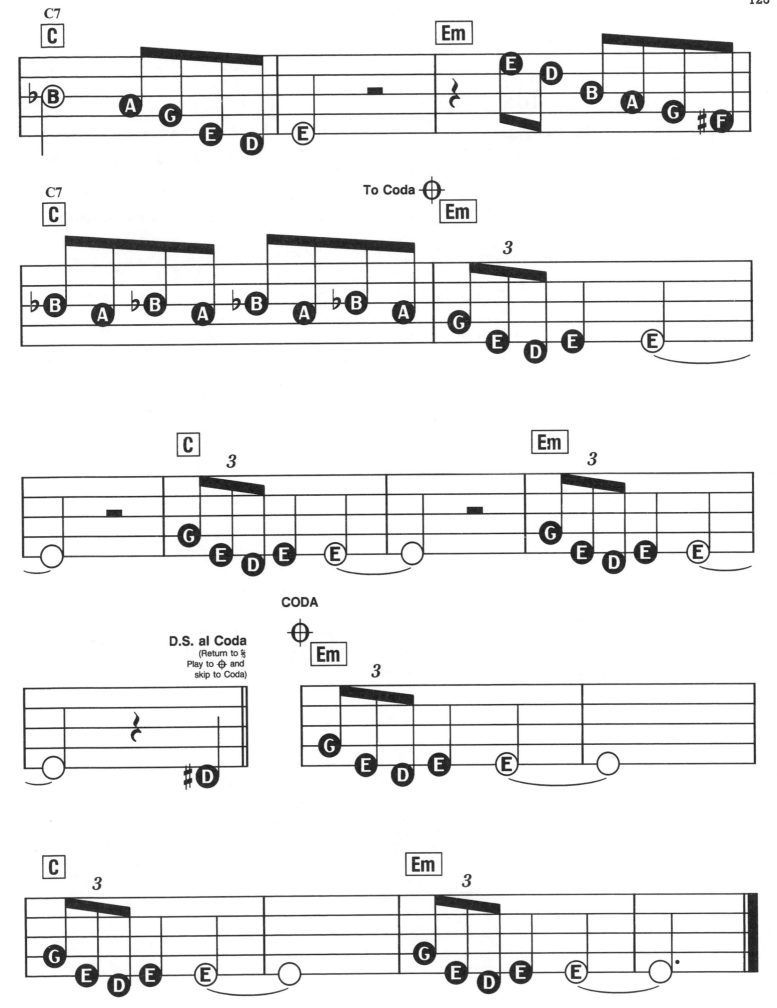

Shallow

from A STAR IS BORN

Registration 4
Rhythm: Folk

Words and Music by Stefani Germanotta,
Mark Ronson, Andrew Wyatt and Anthony Rossomando

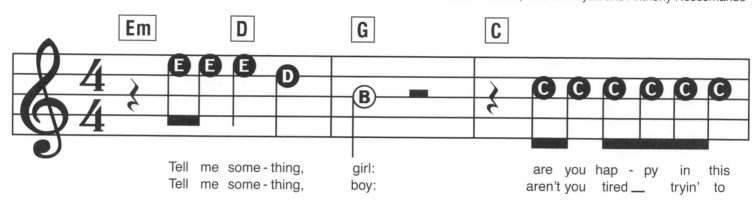

Tell me some - thing, girl: are you hap - py in this
Tell me some - thing, boy: aren't you tired ___ tryin' to

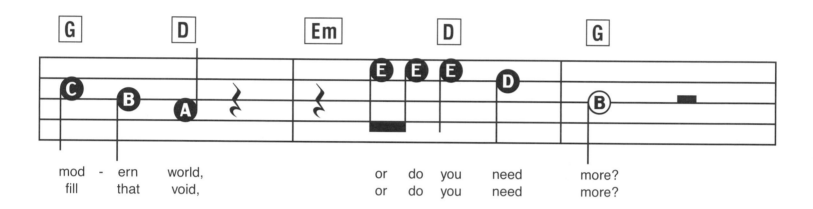

mod - ern world, or do you need more?
fill that void, or do you need more?

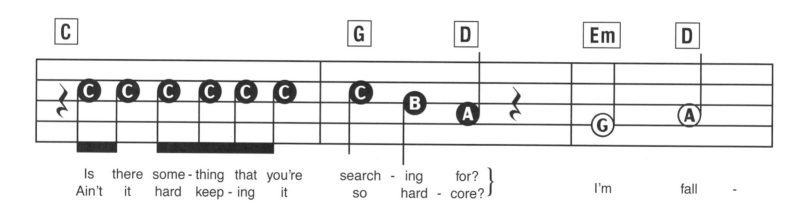

Is there some - thing that you're search - ing for? }
Ain't it hard keep - ing it so hard - core? }
I'm fall -

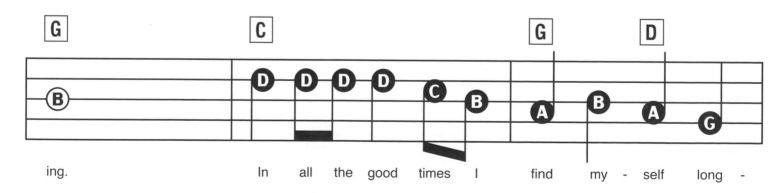

ing. In all the good times I find my - self long -

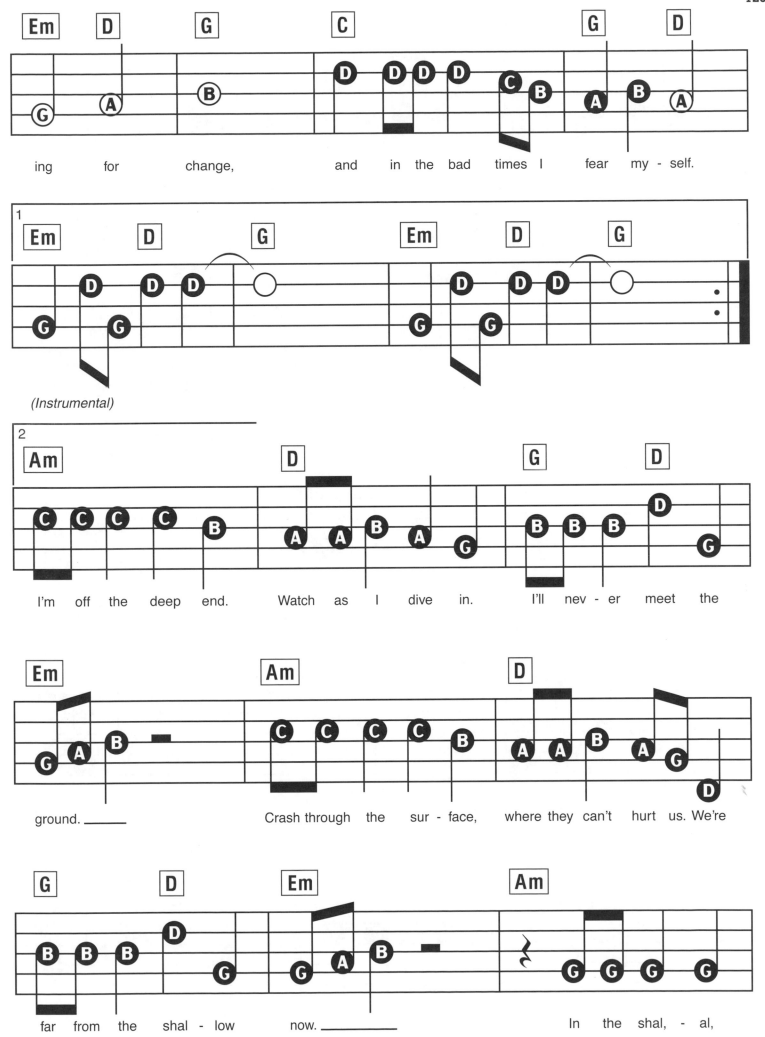

ing   for   change,   and   in the bad   times I   fear   my - self.

(Instrumental)

I'm off   the deep   end.   Watch as   I   dive   in.   I'll nev - er   meet   the

ground. _____   Crash through   the sur - face,   where they can't   hurt us. We're

far from the shal - low   now. _____   In   the shal, - al,

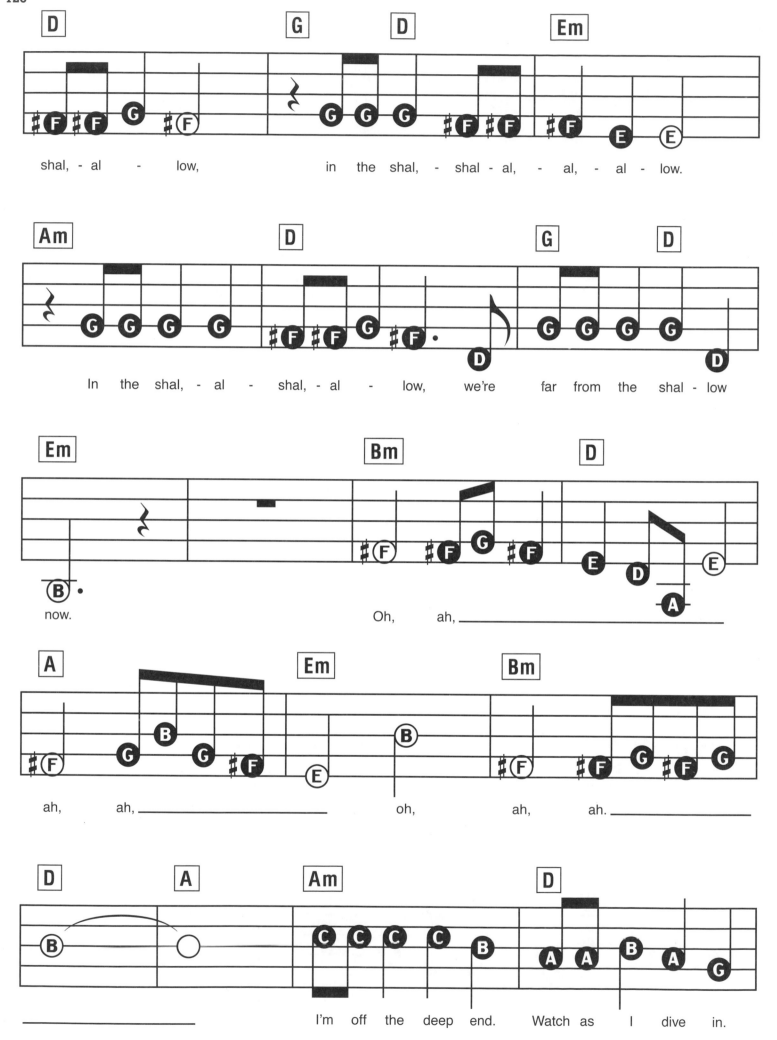

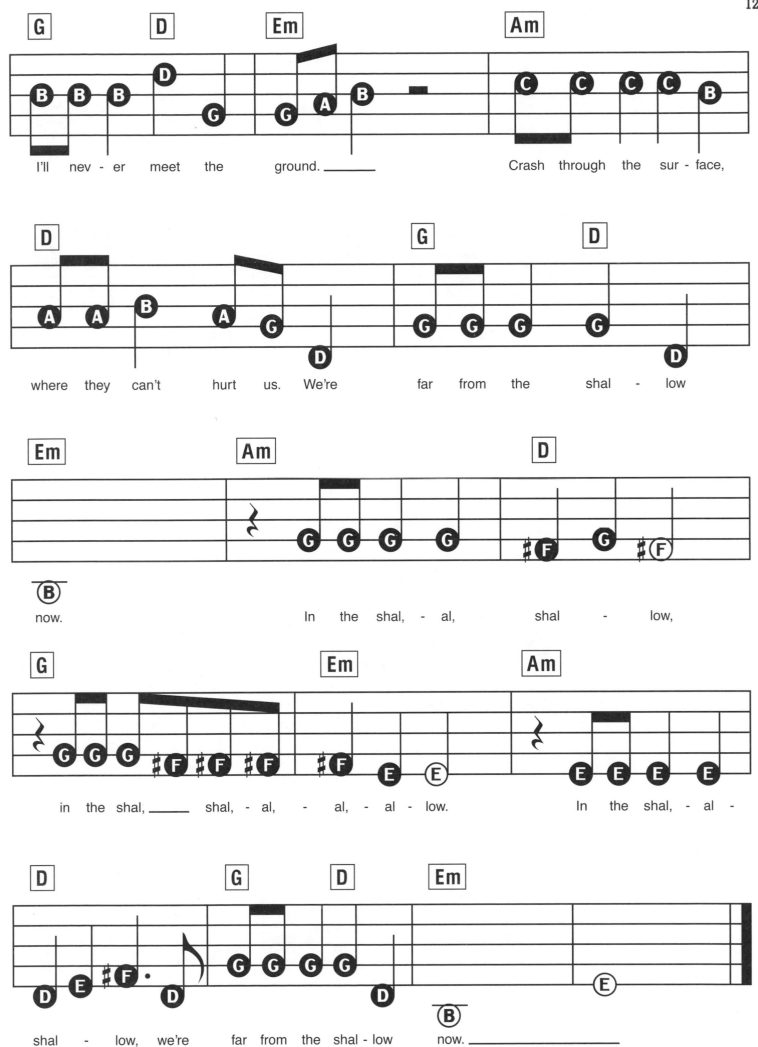

Smoke on the Water

Registration 2
Rhythm: 8 Beat or Rock

Words and Music by Ritchie Blackmore,
Ian Gillan, Roger Glover,
Jon Lord and Ian Paice

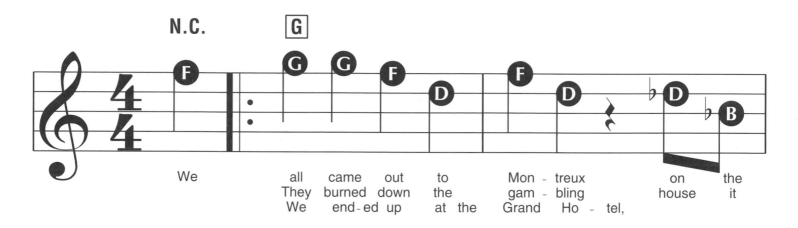

N.C.   G   F   F

We all came out to Mon - treux on the
They burned down the gam - bling house it
We end - ed up at the Grand Ho - tel,

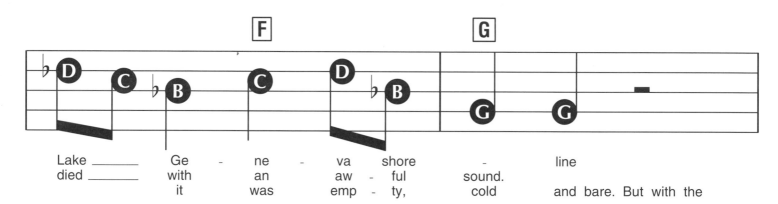

F   G

Lake _____ Ge - ne - va shore - line
died _____ with an aw - ful sound.
it was emp - ty, cold and bare. But with the

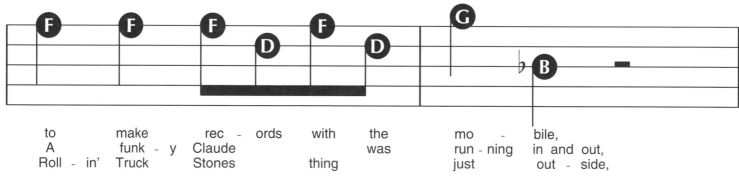

G

to make rec - ords with the mo - bile,
A funk - y Claude was run - ning in and out,
Roll - in' Truck Stones thing just out - side,

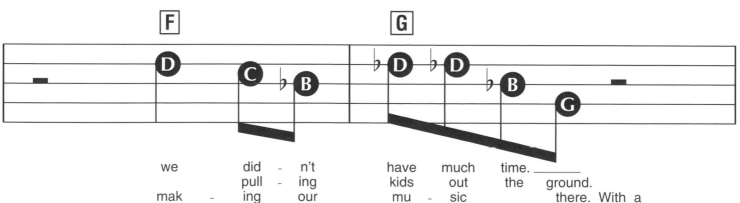

F   G

we did - n't have much time. _____
pull - ing kids out the ground.
mak - ing our mu - sic there. With a

129

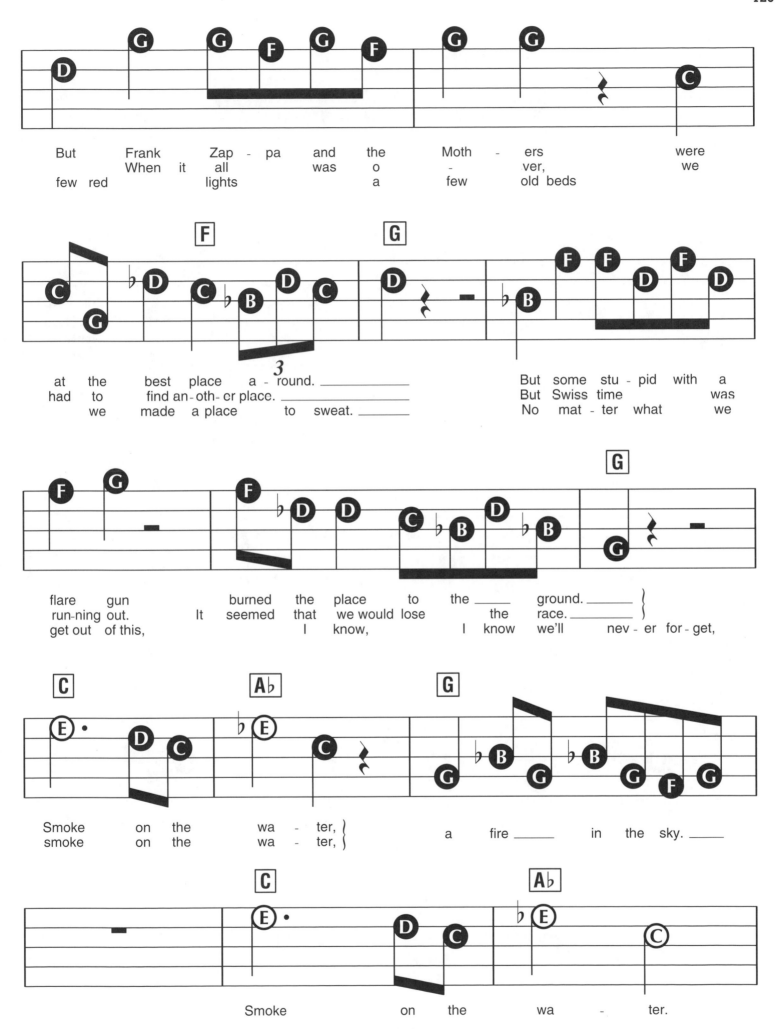

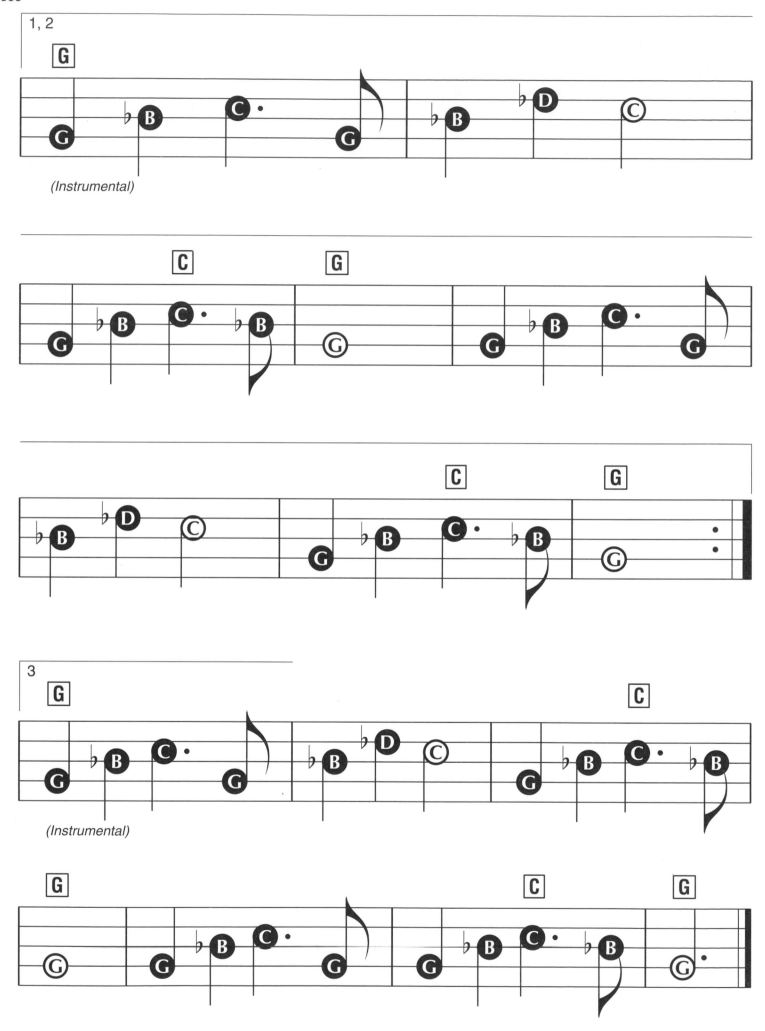

Sweet Caroline

Registration 2
Rhythm: Swing or Fox Trot

Words and Music by
Neil Diamond

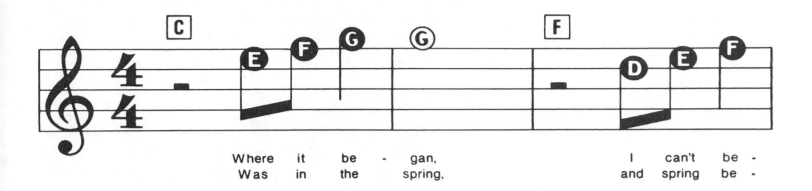

Where it be - gan, I can't be -
Was in the spring, and spring be -

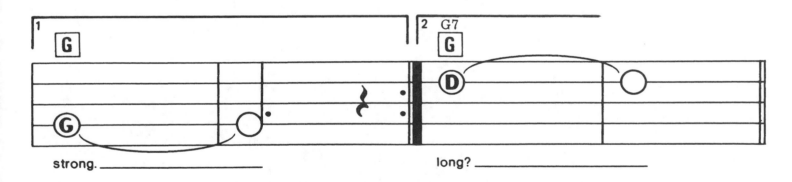

gin to know - in', but then I know it's grow - in'
came the sum - mer, who'd have be - lieved you'd come a -

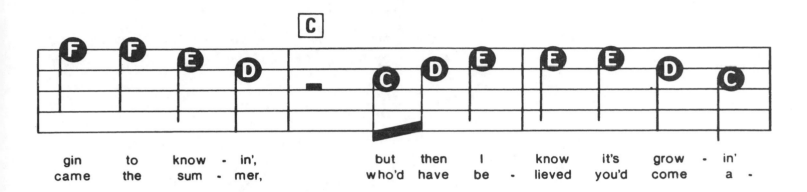

strong. _____ long? _____

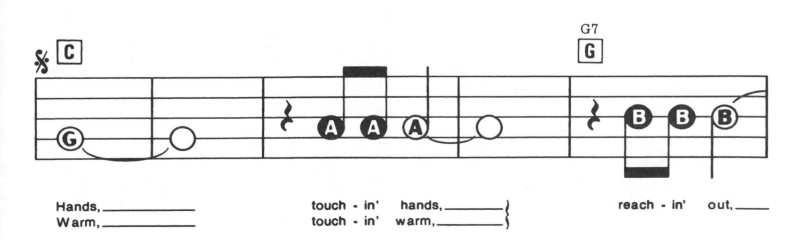

Hands, _____ touch - in' hands, _____ reach - in' out, _____
Warm, _____ touch - in' warm, _____

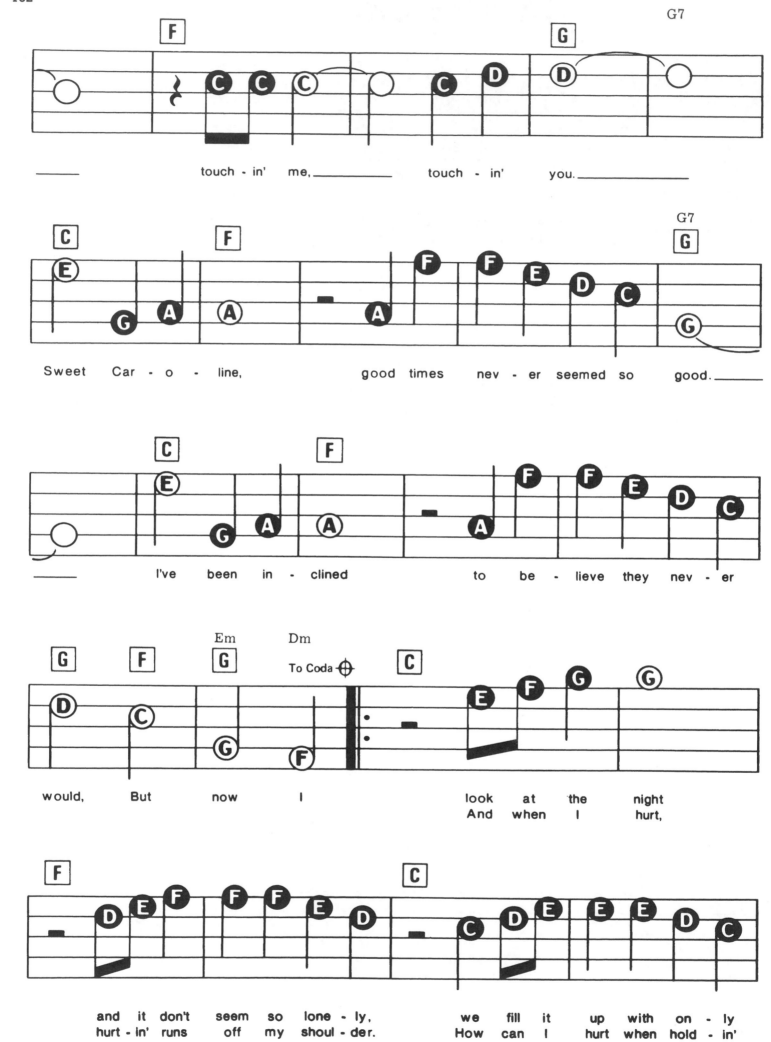

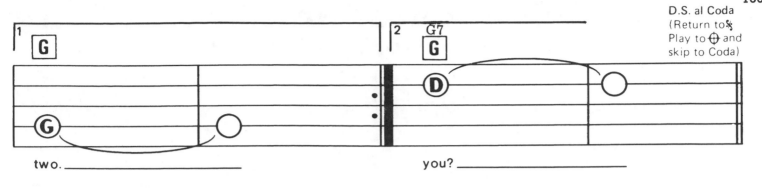

two. _____ you? _____

D.S. al Coda
(Return to %
Play to ⊕ and
skip to Coda)

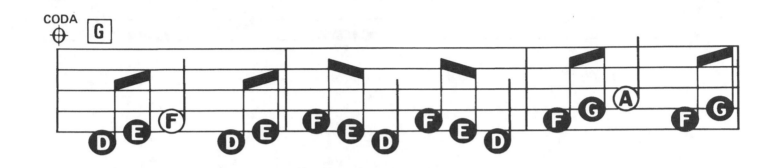

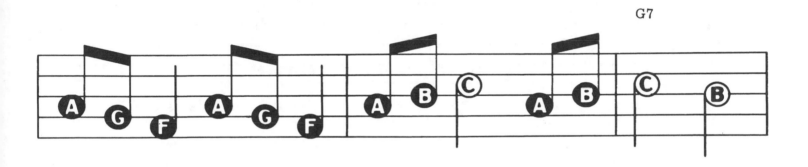

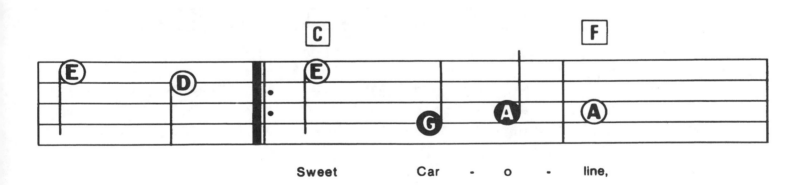

Sweet   Car - o - line,

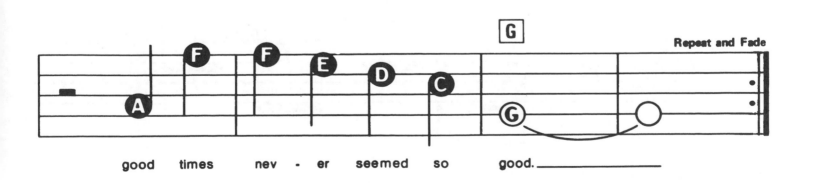

good   times   nev - er   seemed   so   good. _____

SpongeBob SquarePants Theme Song
from SPONGEBOB SQUAREPANTS

Registration 1
Rhythm: Rock

Words and Music by Mark Harrison,
Blaise Smith, Stephen M. Hillenburg
and Derek Drymon

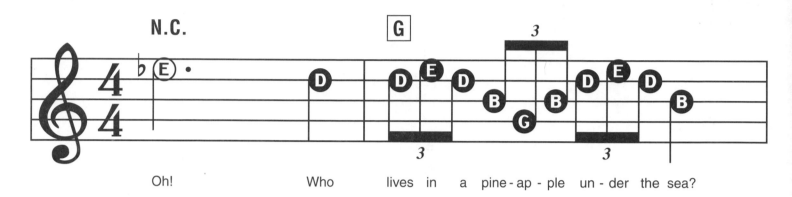

Oh!   Who   lives   in   a   pine - ap - ple   un - der   the   sea?

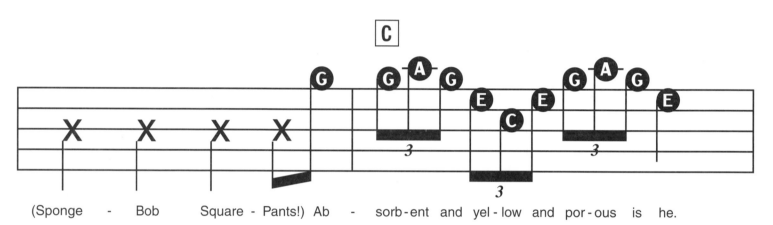

(Sponge - Bob   Square - Pants!)   Ab - sorb - ent   and   yel - low   and   por - ous   is   he.

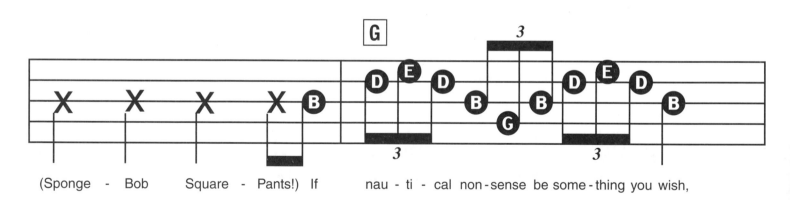

(Sponge - Bob   Square - Pants!)   If   nau - ti - cal   non - sense   be   some - thing   you   wish,

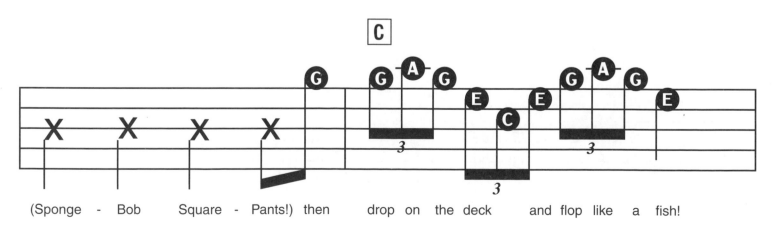

(Sponge - Bob   Square - Pants!)   then   drop   on   the   deck   and   flop   like   a   fish!

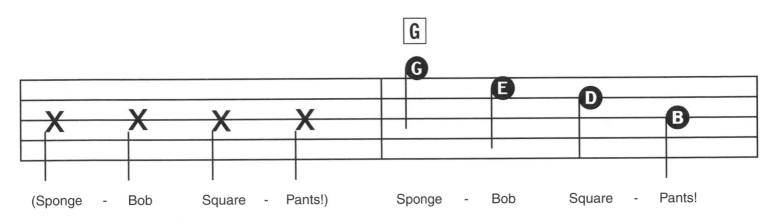

(Sponge - Bob Square - Pants!) Sponge - Bob Square - Pants!

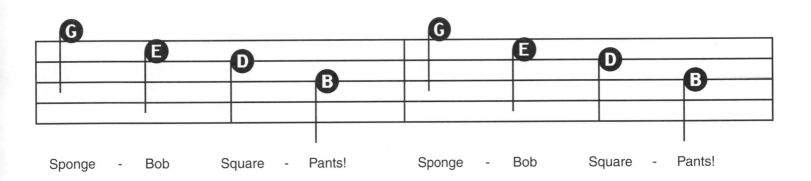

Sponge - Bob Square - Pants! Sponge - Bob Square - Pants!

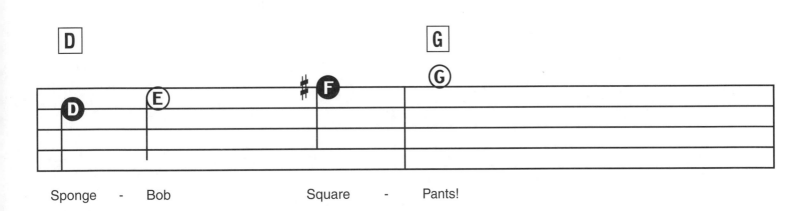

Sponge - Bob Square - Pants!

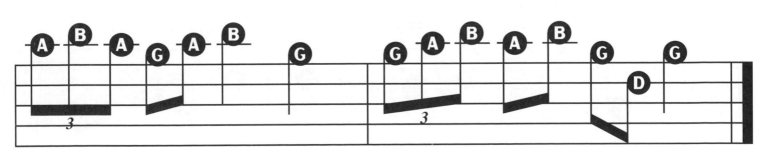

(Instrumental)

Star Wars
(Main Theme)
from STAR WARS: A NEW HOPE

Registration 2
Rhythm: March

Music by John Williams

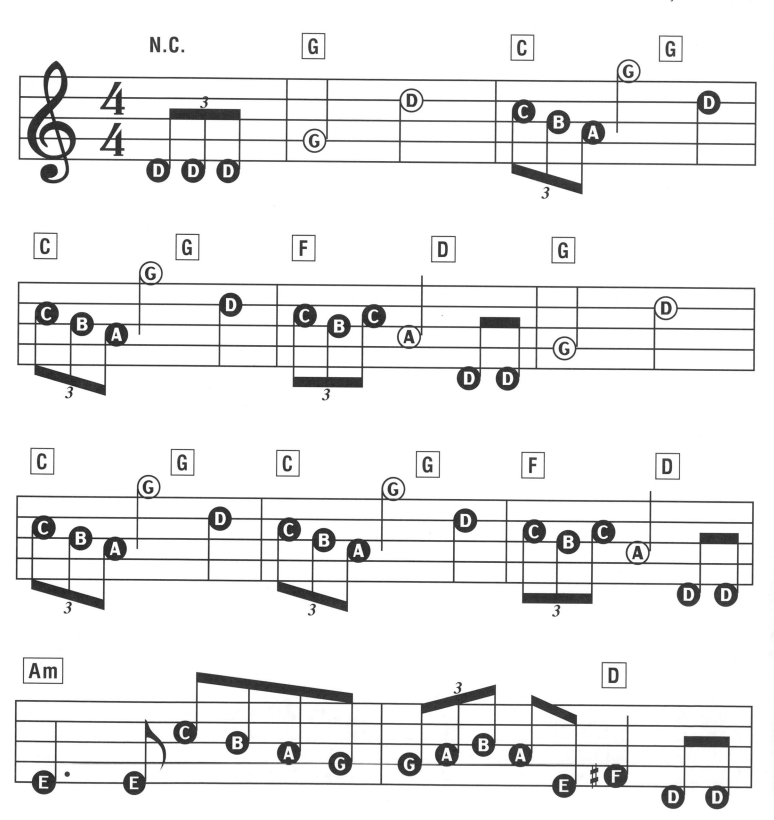

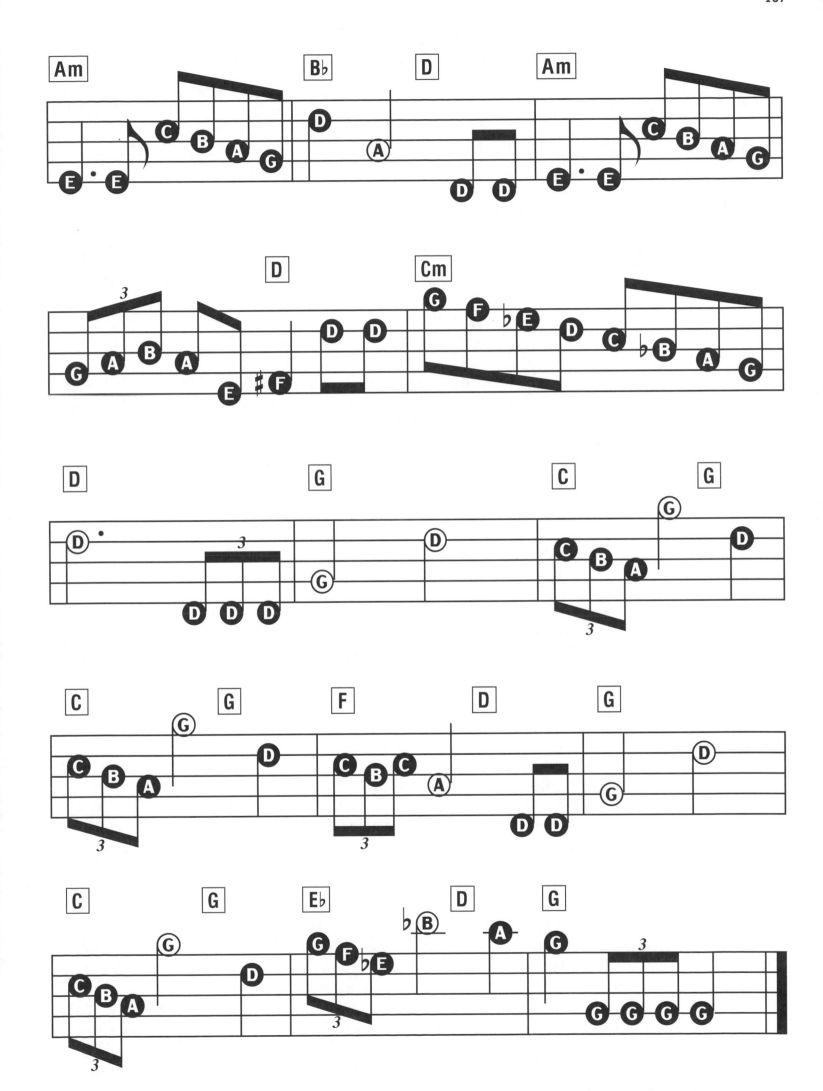

A Thousand Years
from the Summit Entertainment film
THE TWILIGHT SAGA: BREAKING DAWN – PART 1

Registration 8
Rhythm: Waltz

Words and Music by David Hodges
and Christina Perri

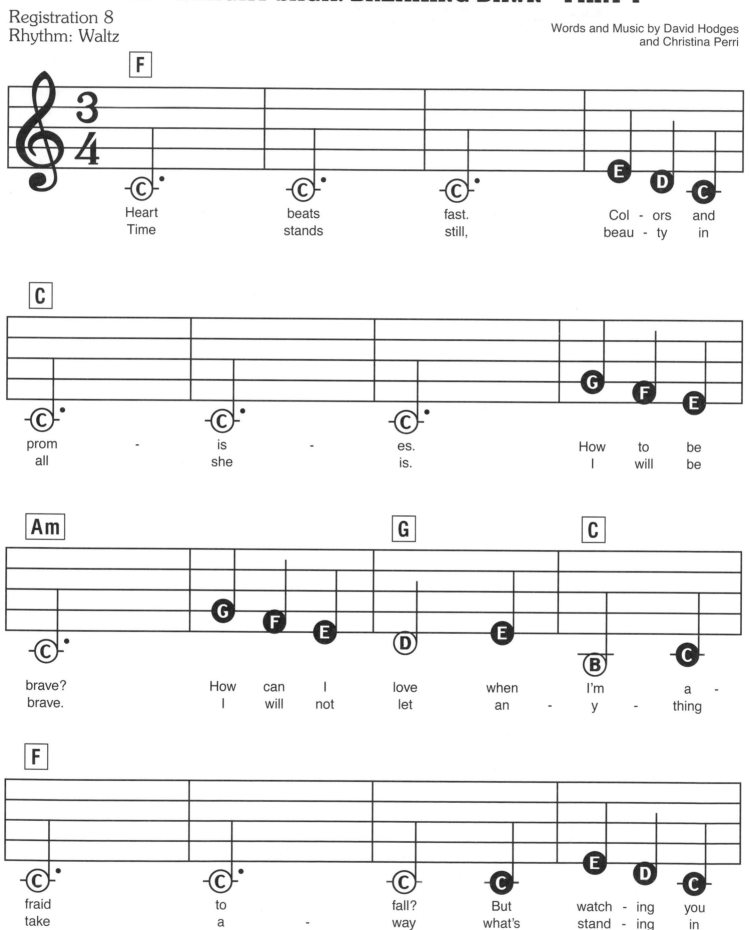

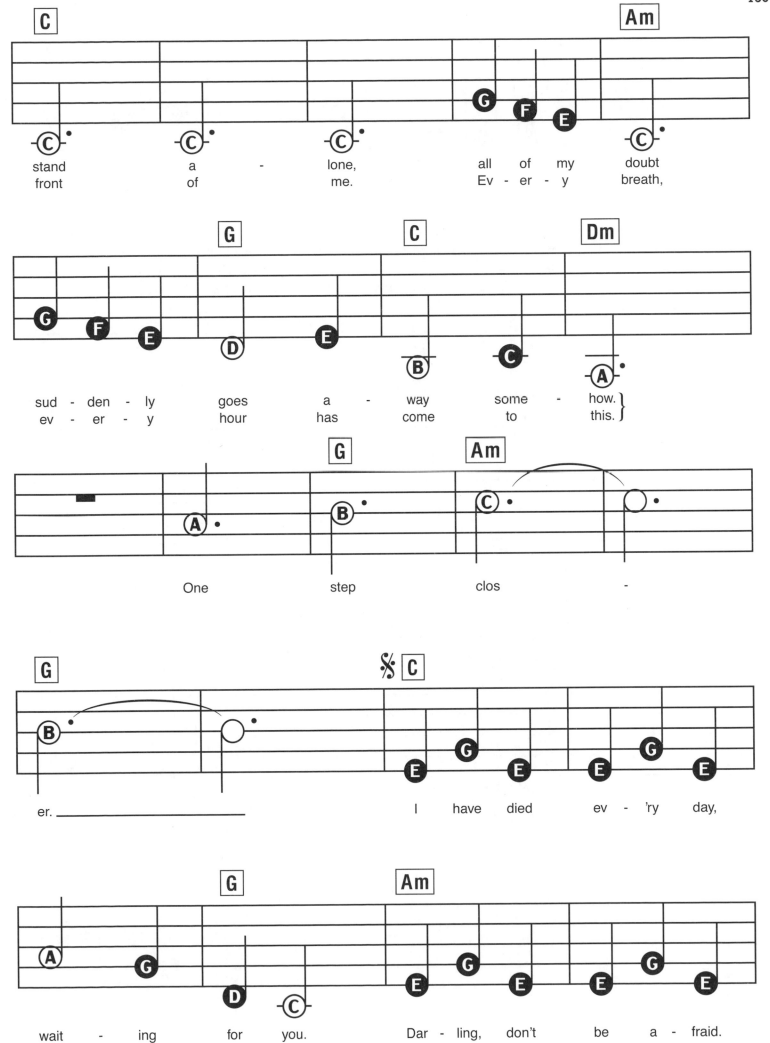

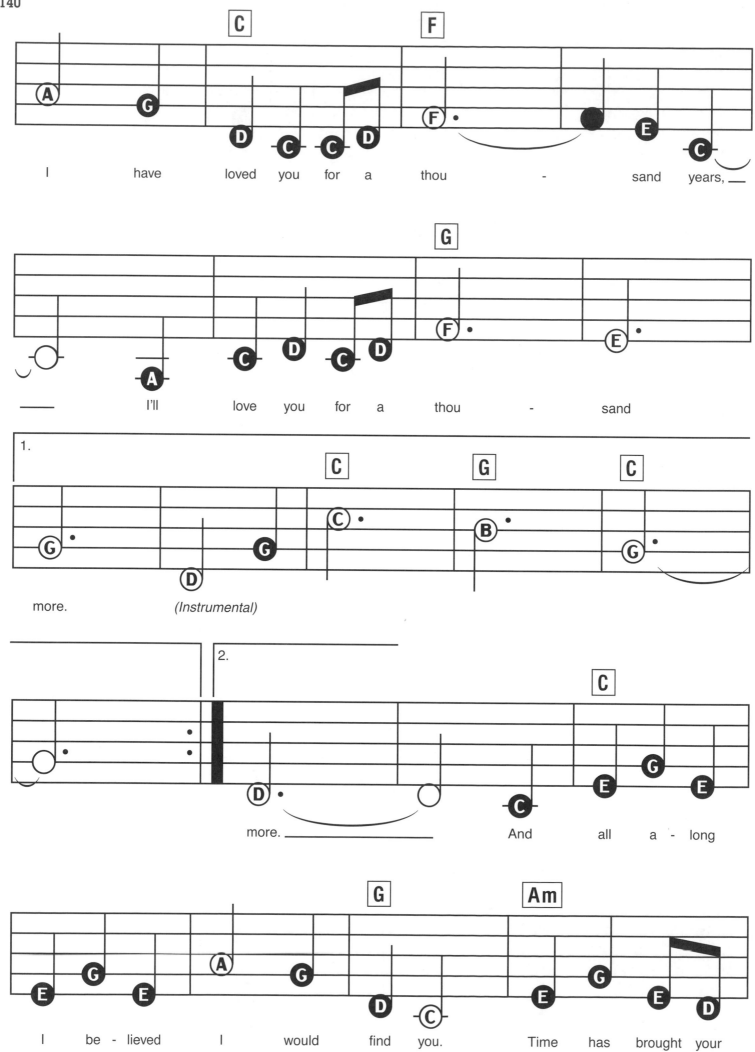

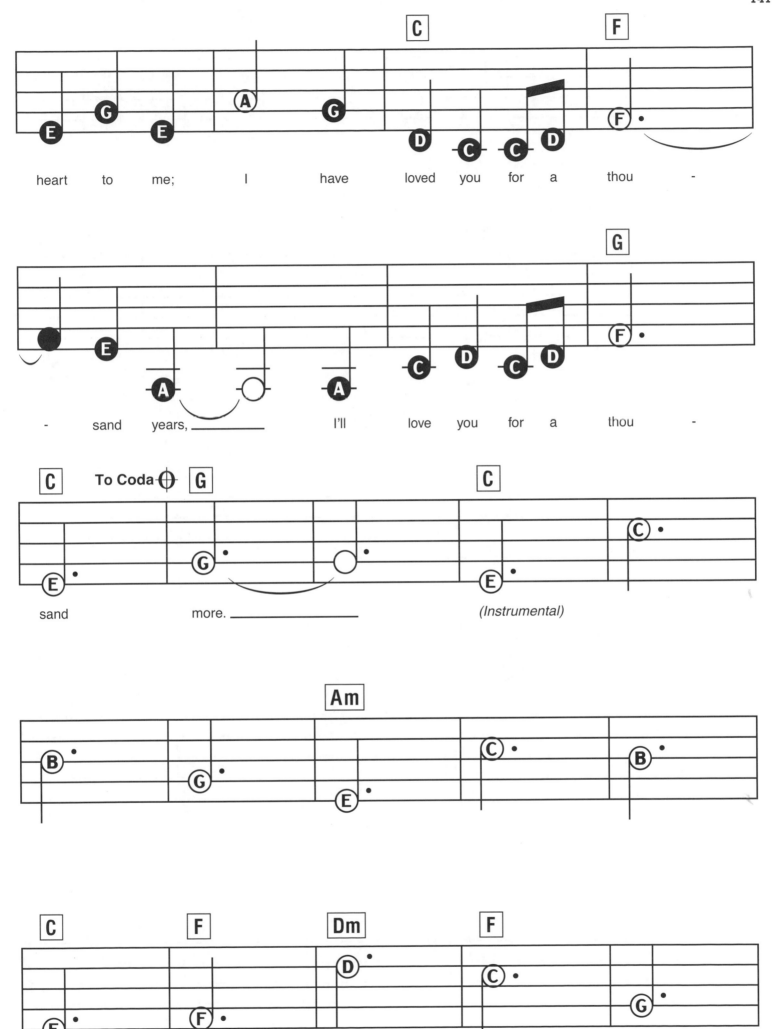

heart to me; I have loved you for a thou-

- sand years, _____ I'll love you for a thou-

sand more. _____ (Instrumental)

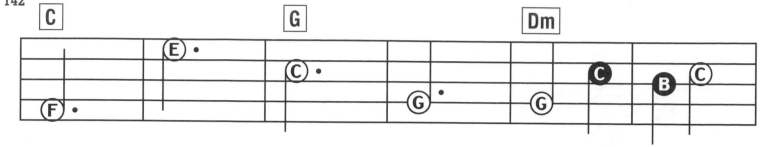

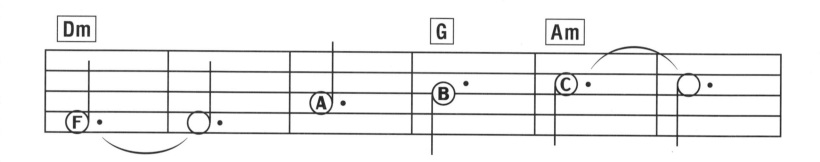

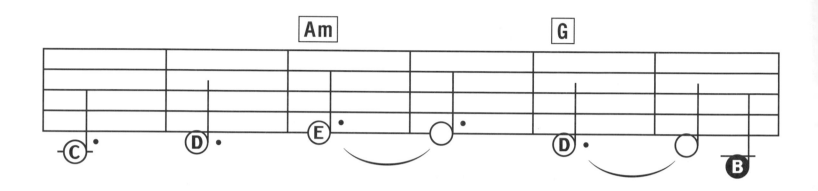

D.S. al Coda
(Return to 𝄋
Play to ⊕ and
Skip to Coda)
(take 2nd ending)

CODA

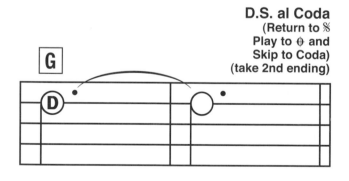

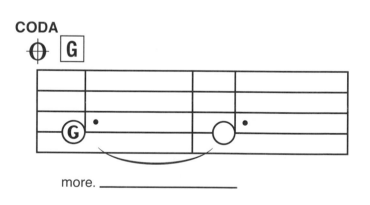

more. _____

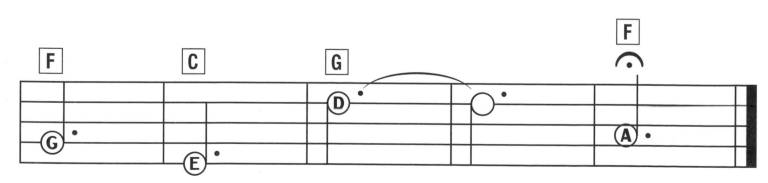

(Instrumental)

VeggieTales Theme Song

Registration 9
Rhythm: March or Fox Trot

Words and Music by Mike Nawrocki
and Lisa Vischer

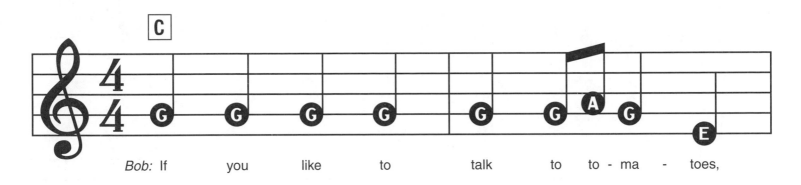

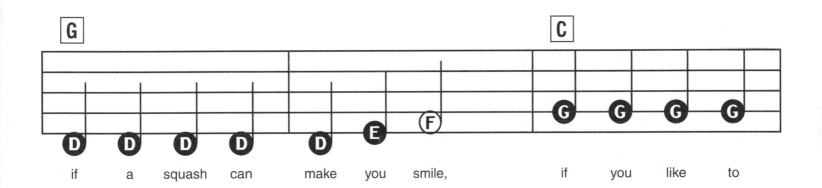

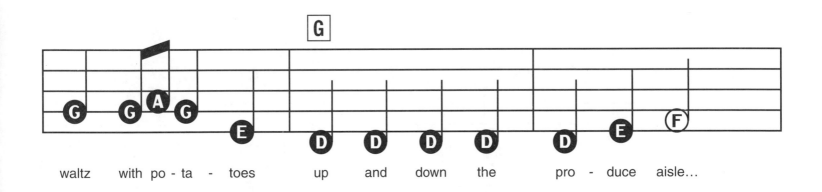

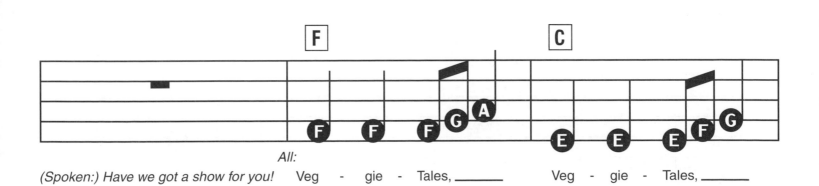

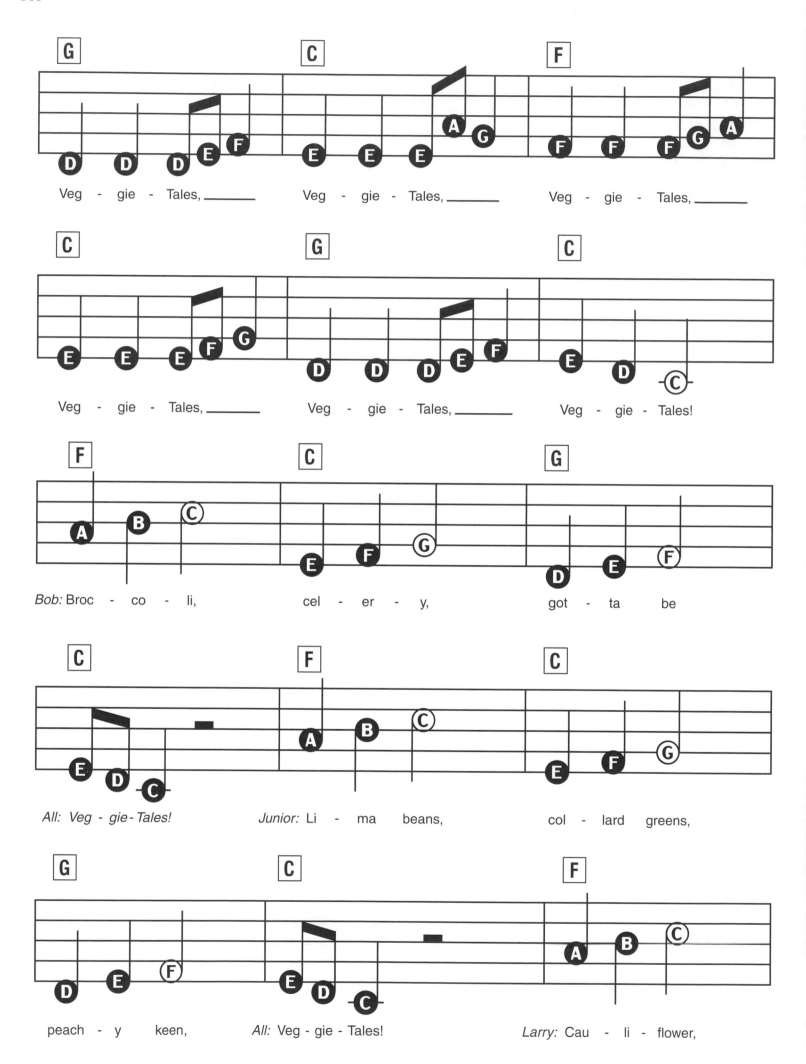

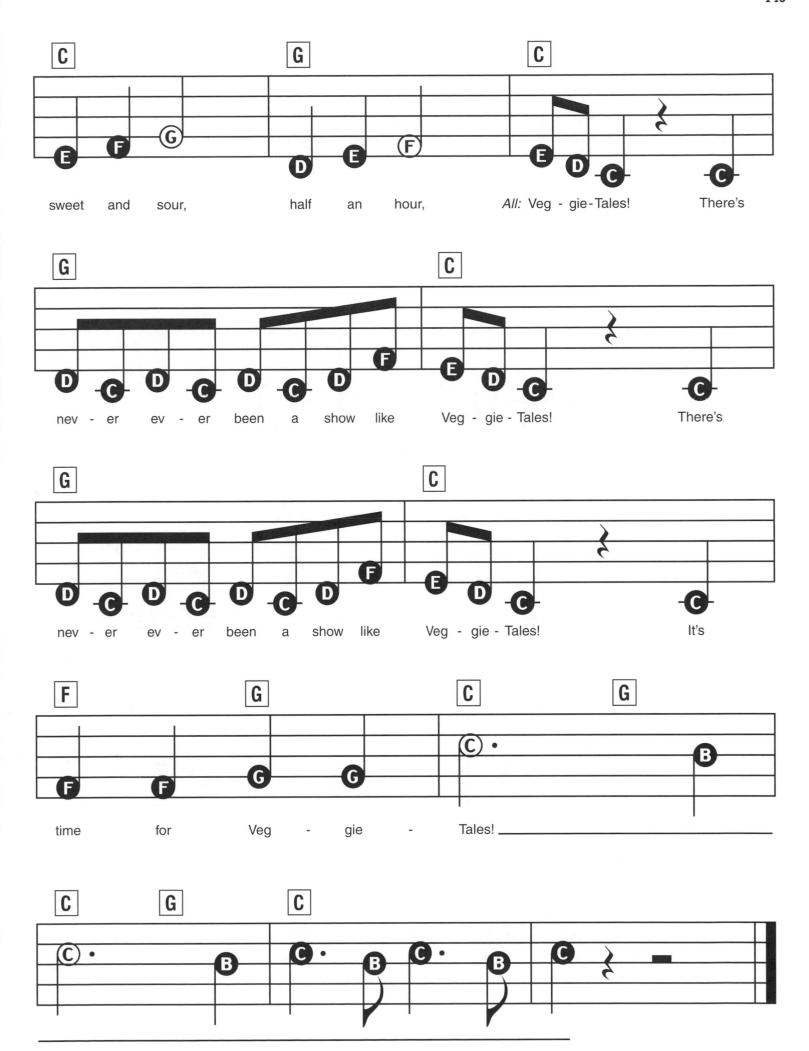

Tomorrow
from the Musical Production ANNIE

Registration 1
Rhythm: Swing or Jazz

Lyric by Martin Charnin
Music by Charles Strouse

The sun - 'll come out_____ to - mor - row,
think - in' a - bout_____ to - mor - row

bet your bot - tom dol - lar that to - mor - row_____
clears a - way the cob - webs and to - the sor - row_____

there'll be sun!_____ Jus'
till there's none,

When I'm stuck with a
day that's gray and lone - ly, I just stick to my

chin and grin and say:_____ Oh! the

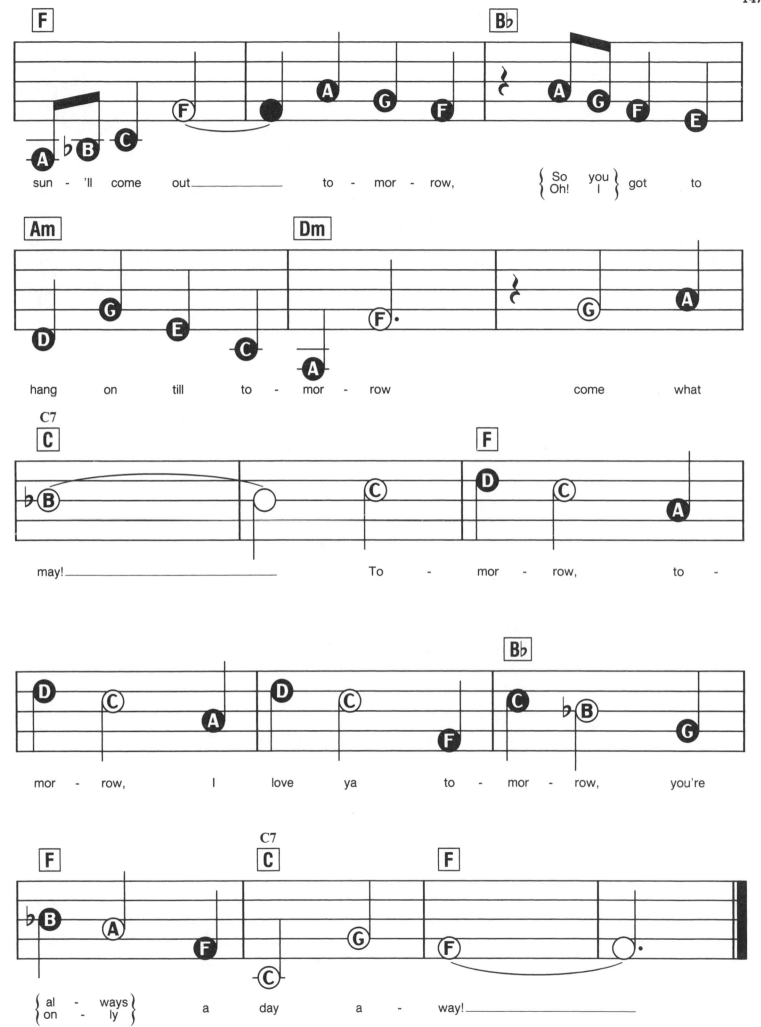

Viva La Vida

Registration 3
Rhythm: Rock or Pop

Words and Music by Guy Berryman,
Jon Buckland, Will Champion
and Chris Martin

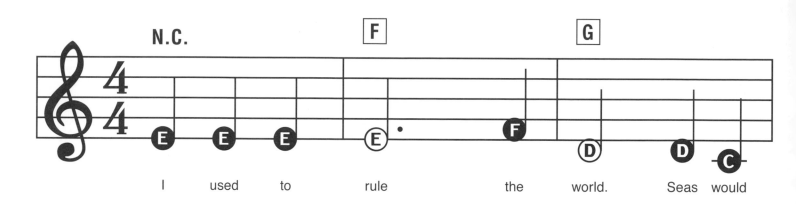

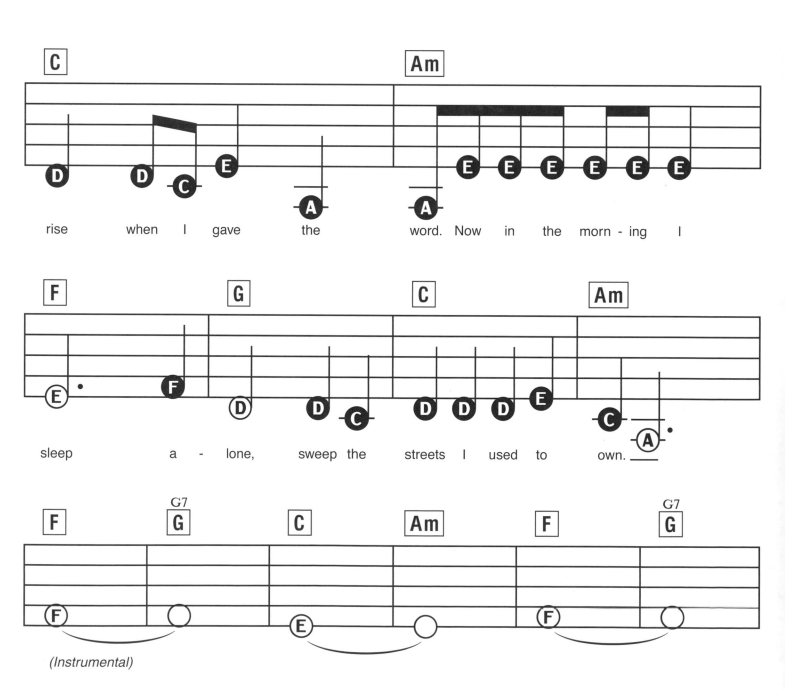

(Instrumental)

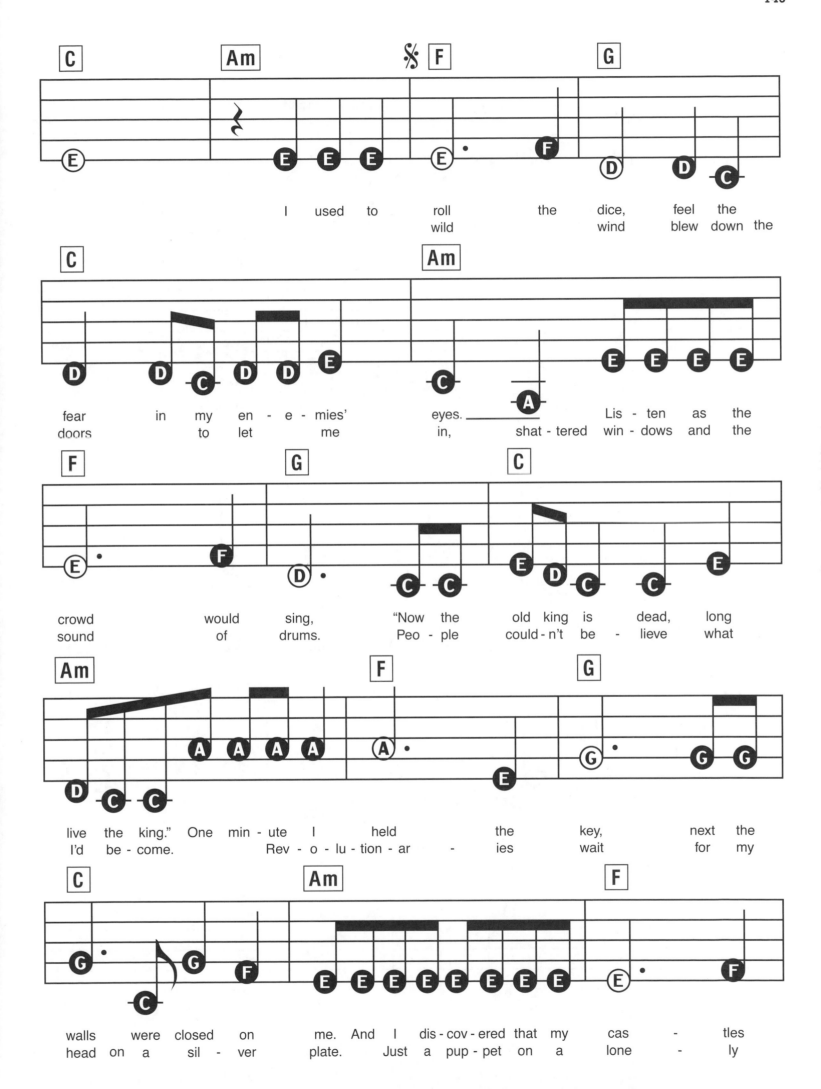

149

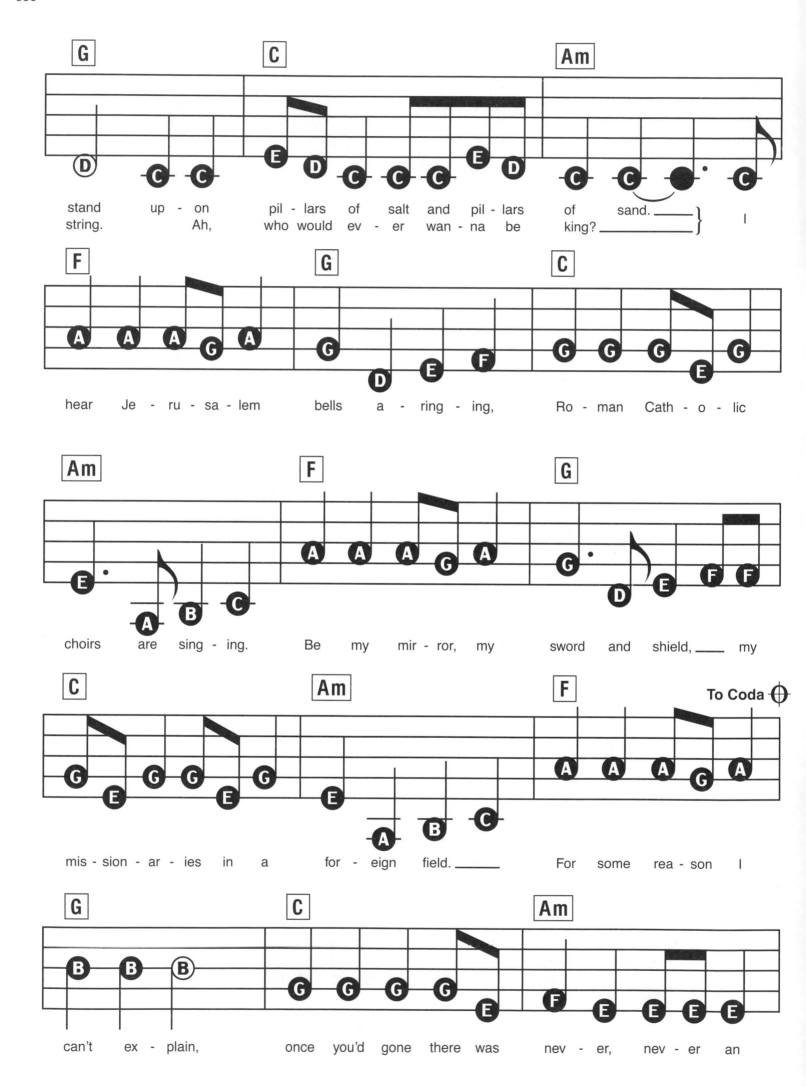

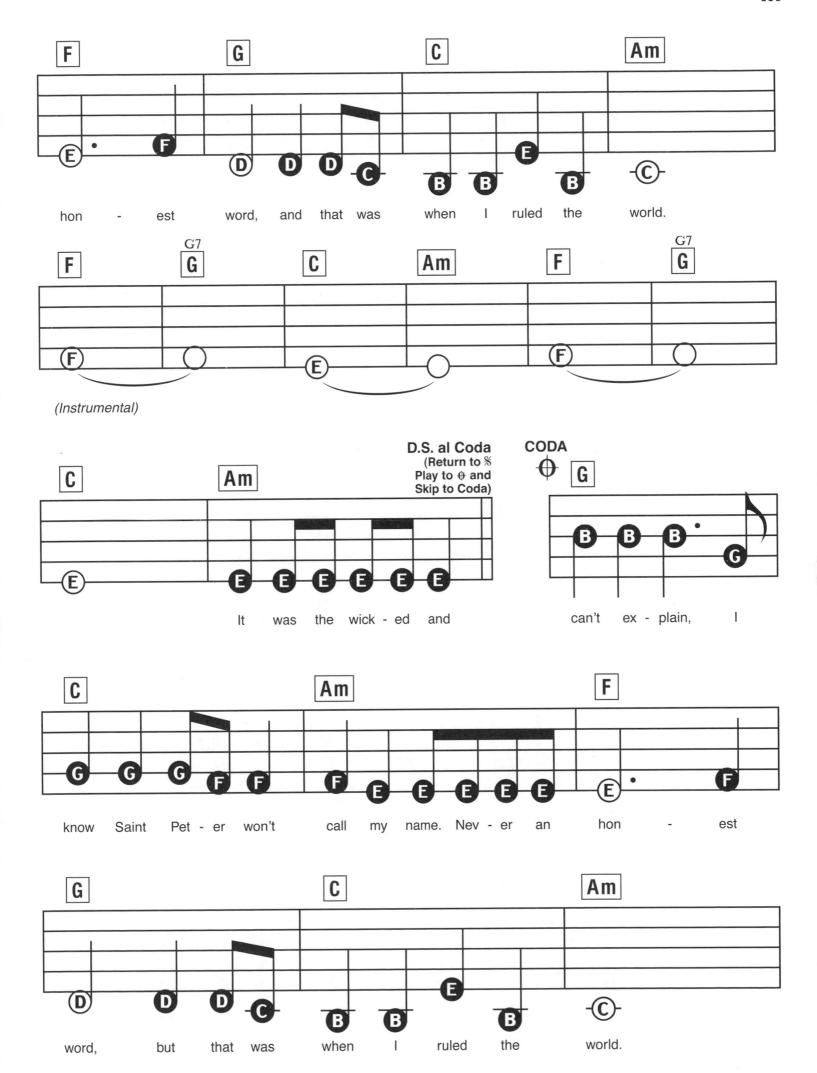

152

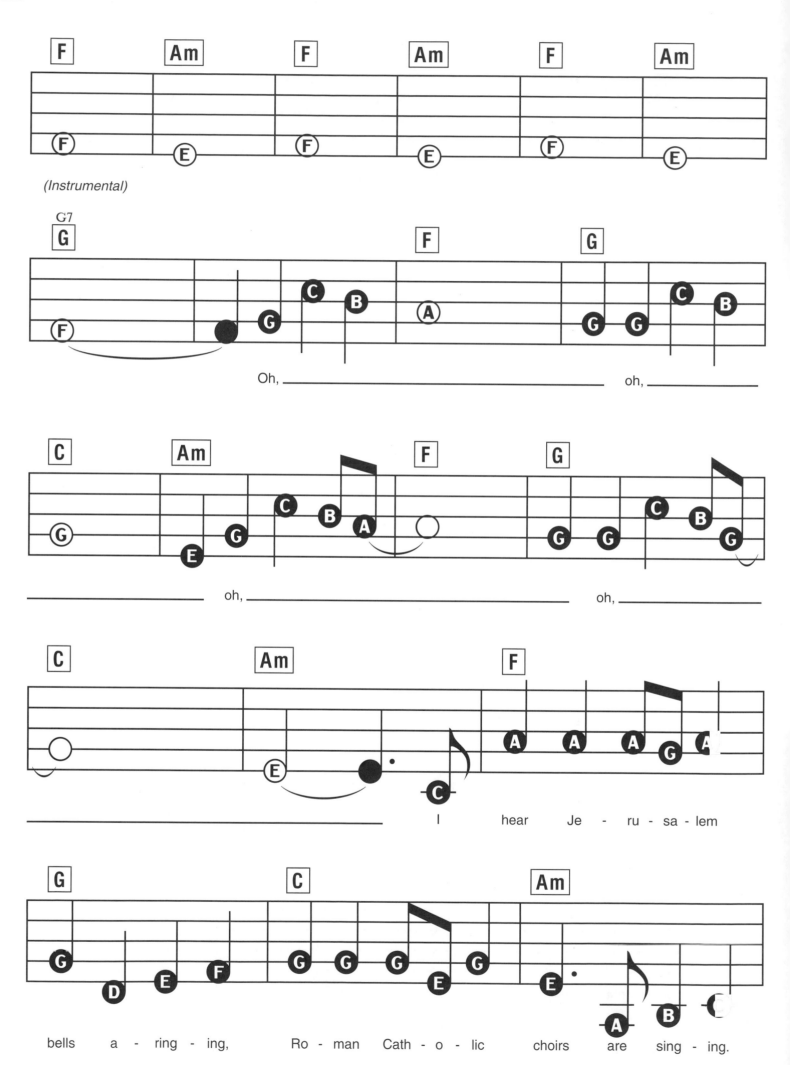

(Instrumental)

Oh, _____ oh, _____

oh, _____ oh, _____

_____ I hear Je - ru - sa - lem

bells a - ring - ing, Ro - man Cath - o - lic choirs are sing - ing.

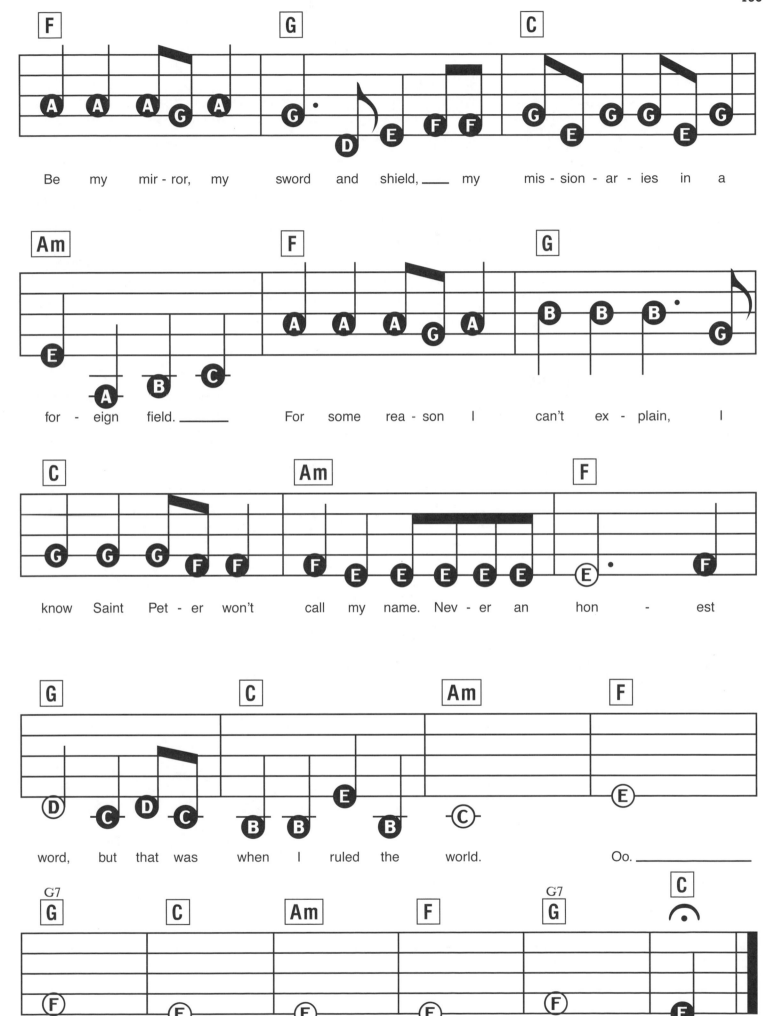

Wellerman

Registration 1
Rhythm: 4-beat

New Zealand Folksong

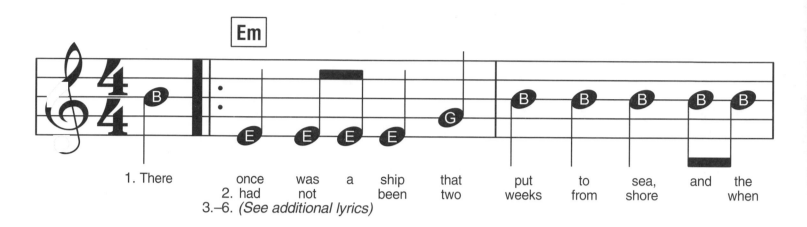

1. There once was a ship that put to sea, and the
2. had not been two weeks from shore, when the
3.–6. *(See additional lyrics)*

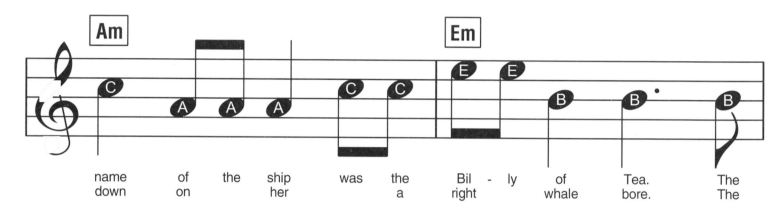

name of the ship was the Bil - ly of Tea. The
down on her was a right whale bore. The

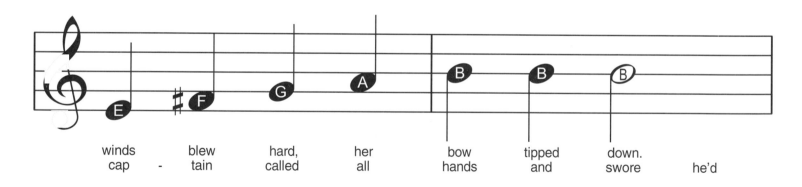

winds blew hard, her bow tipped and down.
cap - tain called her all hands and swore he'd

Chorus

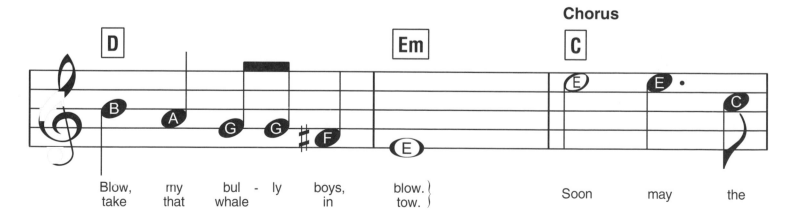

Blow, my bul - ly boys, blow.
take that whale in tow.

Soon may the

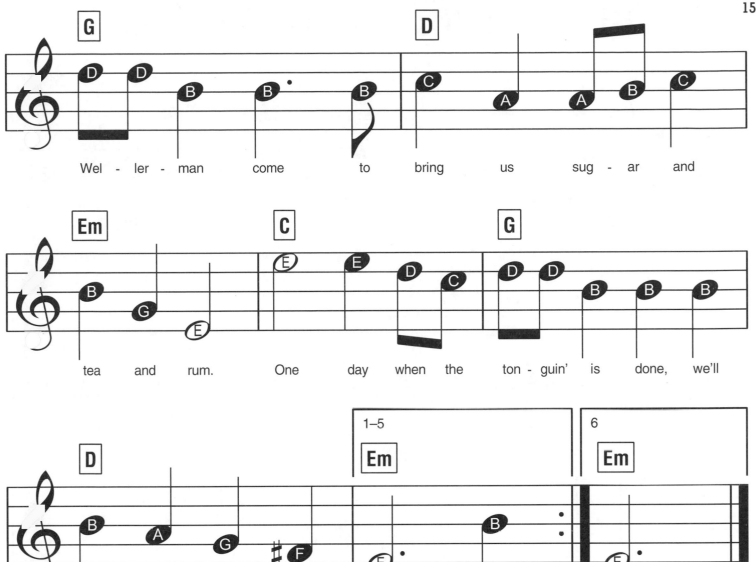

Additional Lyrics

3. Before the boat had hit the water,
   The whale's tail came up and caught her.
   All hands to the side, harpooned and fought her
   When she dived down below.
   Chorus

4. No line was cut, no whale was freed.
   The Captain's mind was not of greed,
   But he belonged to the whaleman's creed.
   She took the ship in tow.
   Chorus

5. For forty days or even more,
   The line went slack, then tight once more.
   All boats were lost (there were only four),
   But still the whale did go.
   Chorus

6. As far as I've heard, the fight's still on.
   The line's not cut and the whale's not gone.
   The Wellerman makes his regular call
   To encourage the Captain, crew and all.
   Chorus

What a Wonderful World

Registration 2
Rhythm: Ballad

Words and Music by George David Weiss
and Bob Thiele

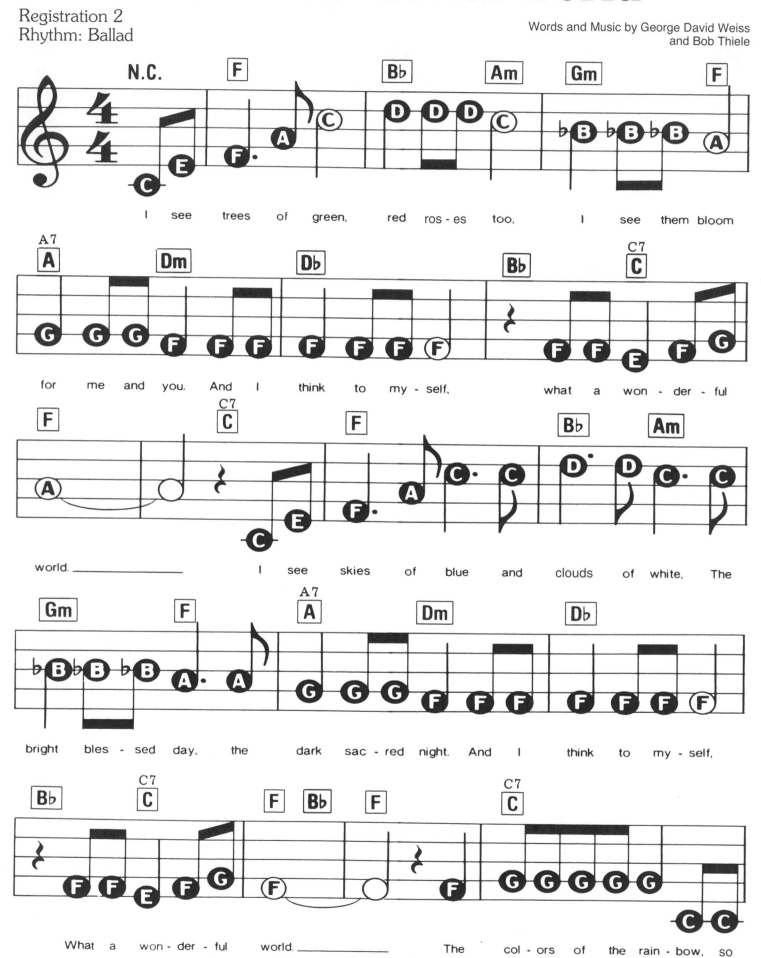

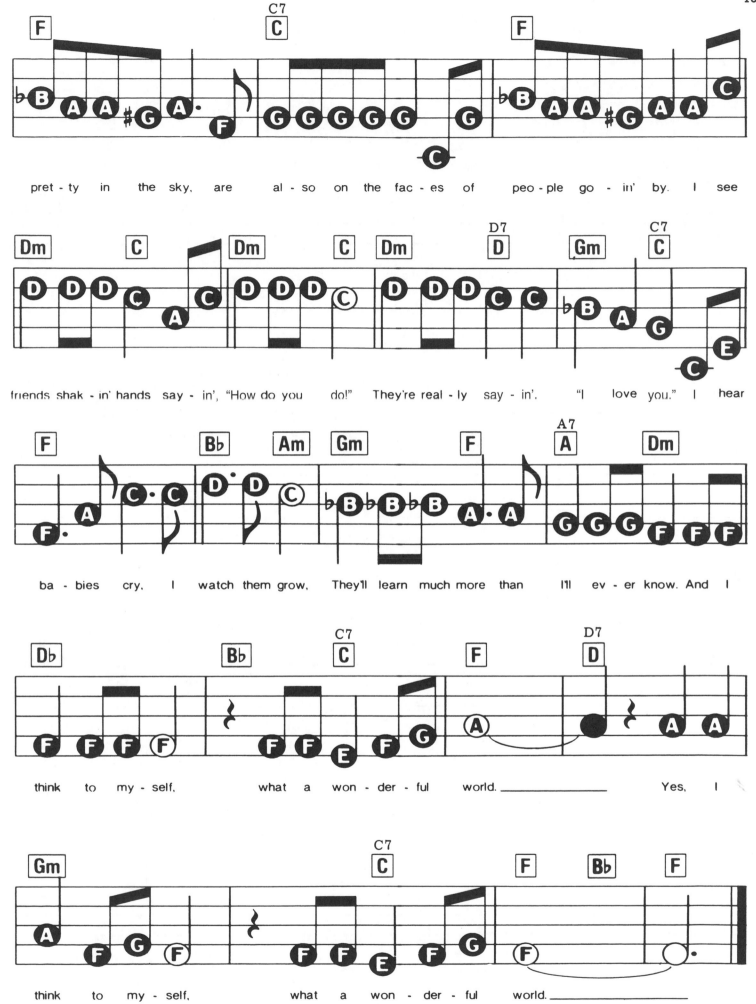

You Are My Sunshine

Registration 4
Rhythm: Fox Trot or Country

Words and Music by
Jimmie Davis

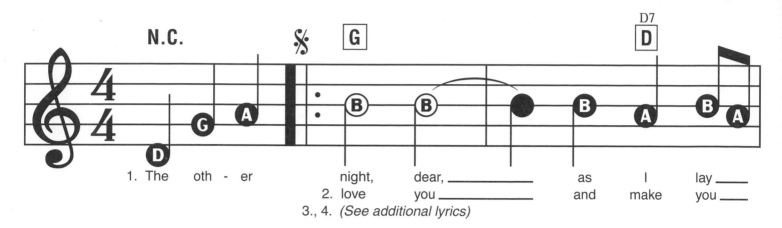

1. The oth - er   night,   dear, _____   as   I   lay _____
2. love   you _____   and   make   you _____
3., 4. *(See additional lyrics)*

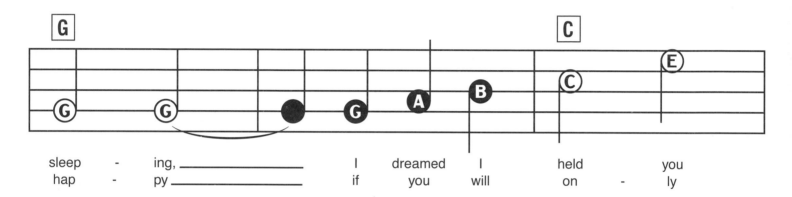

sleep - ing, _____   I   dreamed   I   held   you
hap - py _____   if   you   will   on - ly

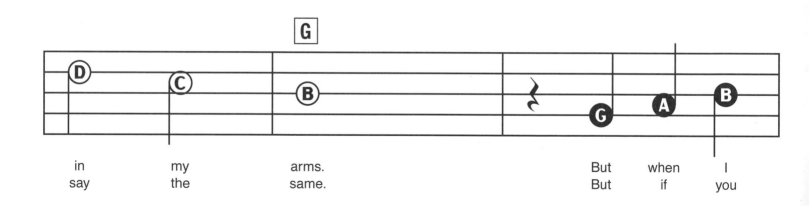

in   my   arms.   But   when   I
say   the   same.   But   if   you

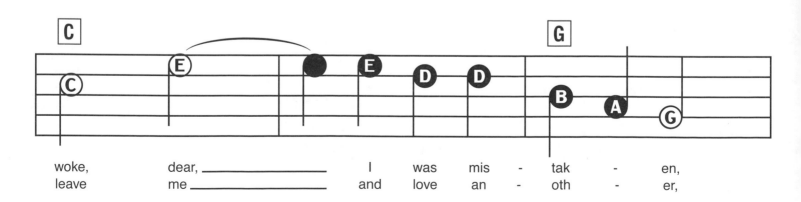

woke,   dear, _____   I   was   mis - tak - en,
leave   me _____   and   love   an - oth - er,

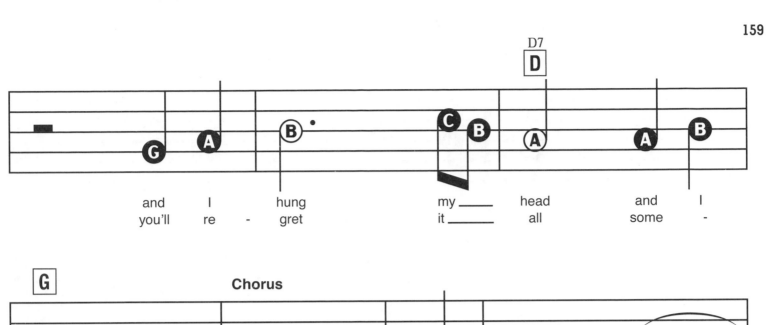

and   I   hung   my ____ head   all   and   I

you'll   re - gret   it _____ all   some -

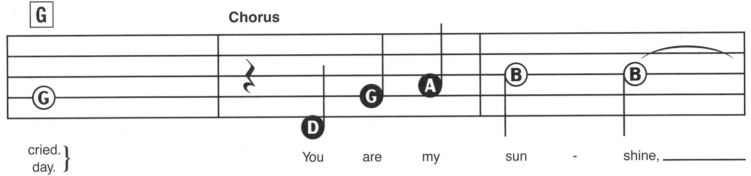

cried. \
day. }   You   are   my   sun - shine, _____

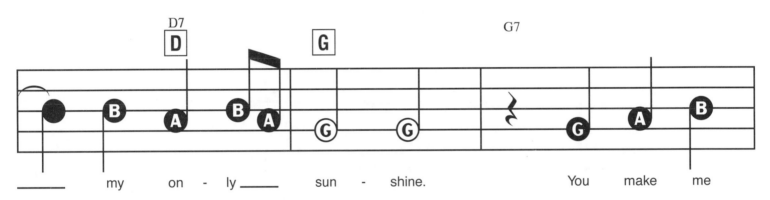

_____ my   on - ly ____ sun - shine.   You   make   me

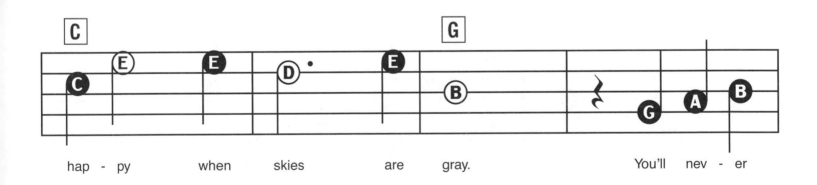

hap - py   when   skies   are   gray.   You'll   nev - er

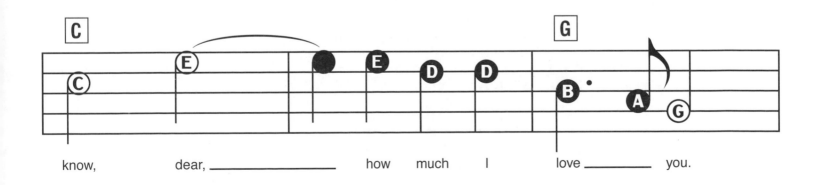

know,   dear, _____ how   much   I   love _____ you.

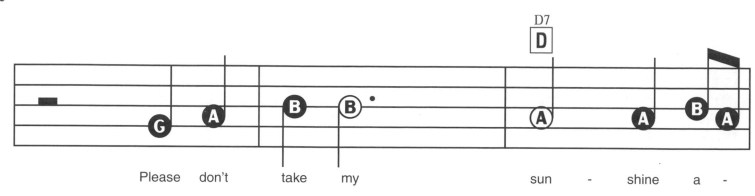

Please don't take my sun - shine a -

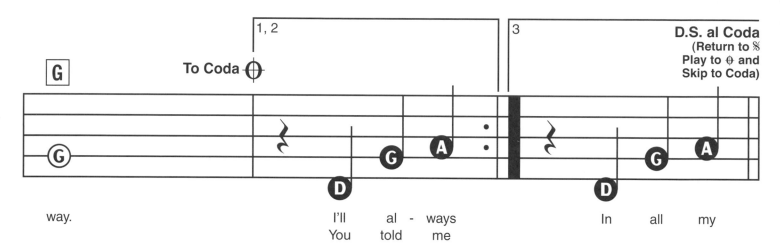

way.

I'll al - ways
You told me

In all my

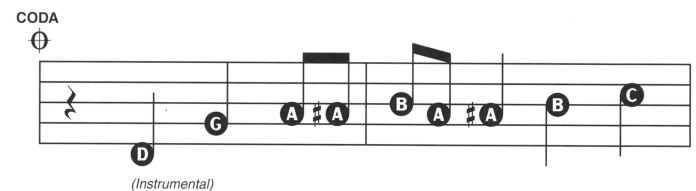

(Instrumental)

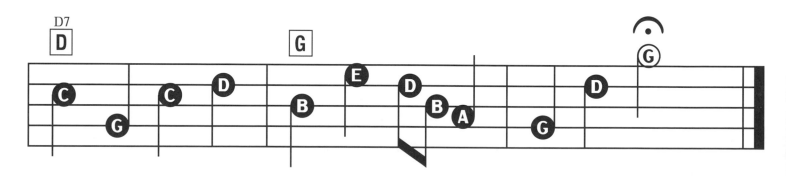

Additional Lyrics

3. You told me once, dear, you really loved me
And no one could come between.
But now you've left me to love another.
You have shattered all of my dreams.
Chorus

4. In all my dreams, dear, you seem to leave me.
When I awake, my poor heart pains.
So won't you come back and make me happy?
I'll forgive, dear; I'll take all the blame.
Chorus